OUTCOME FUNDING

A New Approach to Targeted Grantmaking

by
Harold S. Williams,
Arthur Y. Webb, and William J. Phillips

- Fourth Edition -

ISBN 0-9629798-5-6

Library of Congress Catalog Card Number 91-62146
Eighth Printing 2012

The Rensselaerville Institute
Delmar, New York, 12054

www.RInstitute.org

OUTCOME FUNDING

A New Approach to Targeted Grantmaking

TABLE OF CONTENTS

PREFACE

"Walk your talk" is the clever if overused admonition which reminds all of us who would preach that at some time we should also practice. Nowhere is the caution more relevant than with writings on organizational development. In the public sector, we are told to do many things--from empowering employees to reinventing government. The problem is not a lack of goals, nor even a lack of strategies. The problem is a lack of tactics. In the fashionable search for strategic principles, we forget that most of our game lies in execution.

Few of us engaged in financial management and allocations in government would question the need for change. Our paper laden and procedurally inclined funding has led us away from the primary principle of public investment: the search for results.

Enter Outcome Funding. This is one of the very few books offering a new approach to a stale practice whose wisdom is proven. Williams, Webb, Phillips, and The Rensselaerville Institute have for seven years honed the applications of Outcome Funding. Indeed, they started long before the book. Good policy, in this book, follows good practice.

For the past two years, we have used Outcome Funding in a variety of social and human service programs in Tennessee. My colleagues and I have found it a highly effective tool. It is no magic wand; it causes us to work both smarter and harder than when following hallowed routines of proposal grading and project monitoring. But the results are well worth the effort. Not only do our state staff like the approach but so, also, do many of our providers. They have long known the difference between counting the number of workshops and asking if anyone who attended a workshop became better.

More recently, we are considering how Outcome Funding principles can help us internally. Specifically, we are looking at how our operating units can justify budget allocations through use of target plans and commitments to results.

I commend this book along with its Outcome Funding approach to all who question the current practice in grantmaking and contracting in the public sector.

David L. Manning, Commissioner
Department of Finance and Administration,
State of Tennessee

INTRODUCTION: Still Trouble in Paradise

In the first edition of Outcome Funding, we called the Introduction, "Trouble in Paradise." The observation still holds. Indeed, in the intervening two years from publication, we have viewed the grantmaking system up close in many forms. Its power to resist change is awesome. At the same time, we have seen some highly effective and energetic people make major strides in reforming grantmaking toward a focus on outcomes. And at a national level, we have seen a variety of movements emerge to push notions of results.

The popular book, *Reinventing Government* by David Osborne and Ted Gaebler, is a strong and eloquent plea to focus on outcomes and to give operating units in the public sector the flexibility to achieve them. The book includes these useful subheadings: What gets measured gets done.... If you don't measure results, you can't tell success from failure....If you can't see success, you can't reward it.

In the first year of the Clinton administration in Washington, we see the challenge accepted at the federal level. Vice President Gore has pledged a full assault on the huge procedural system set up for procurement, noting that nine pages of specifications and guidelines now attend the acquisition of simple glass ashtrays. Meanwhile, a US Senate Bill entitled The Government Performance and Results Act, first introduced in 1990, moves ever closer to Congressional approval. This bill would have federal agencies be accountable for outcome standards in what amounts to performance-based budgeting. At the state and local levels, even more progress has been made. While enormous hurdles of vested interest push against the move to outcomes, its time is now.

We view Outcome Funding as the companion pursuit to

greater effectiveness and efficiency within government. While many of us think of government at all levels as a provider of programs and an enforcer of regulations, perhaps its greatest single function is to distribute money. From public assistance to housing, government is as likely to achieve public benefits by funding other agents to provide and deliver its services as to do it directly. Cities, villages, towns, and counties are all bankrolled to carry out purposes of federal and state government, as are thousands of non-profit groups. Increasingly, for-profit businesses are also getting into this act as well.

In virtually any area, government provides funds for programs; it does so by using a hallowed process anchored in preparation and review of one document. It is called "The Proposal." From needs statement to line-item budget, both its format and content have remained remarkably unchanged over many years. When government funds its own departments or agencies--an equally sacred dance--the budgeting process comes into play. This financial and political sport is also slow to change. Even with the options in use--including zero based budgeting--the basic mindset remains intact.

Requests for Proposals or "RFPs" are a routine of public life. For applicants, the prescribed role is that of supplicant. Great care is taken to craft not only the proper sentences, but the right concepts to conform to what is expected. Proposal review is equally precise--points are allocated to each document section, with the winner determined by numerical count, with a dollop of political or social or economic clout occasionally added. While the measures are less clear, the same general process occurs in budget-seeking within organizations.

This system does have its virtues. For the applicant, it is both understandable and predictable. The function of getting the money is neatly separable from other organizational activities. For the funder, the system offers a form of accountability and considerable control, as well as the appearance of rationality in resource allocation. The process is defensible, even to those who do not get money.

Beneath this placid surface, the process is fatally flawed. Simply put, the proposal is an extraordinarily weak device used to accomplish two critical purposes. The first is to enable public sector investors to understand just what it is that they are buying, and the likelihood of getting it. The second is to enable implementors to have in hand what they need to manage projects to achieve results. Most proposal content is virtually irrelevant to these key purposes. An awesome gap can exist between a Grade A proposal and a Grade A project. And for the implementor, the proposal is often a way to get money, but seldom an effective road map for spending it.

For supplicant and funder alike, proposal development and review is a congenial process. It is also, however, a mild and perhaps unintentional form of collusion, in which each side gives the other something less than it really needs.

At present, the public-sector funding process might well be characterized as "Input Funding: Getting to Compliance." If a group seeking to place unemployed persons in unsubsidized jobs indicates that they will conduct fourteen workshops for 150 persons, the audit function can and will ensure that this number of workshops were held, and said number of participants attended. The problem is a basic one: our eyes are on the wrong target. We should be far more concerned with how many workshop participants got and kept a job, than with the number of sessions that were held.

The public-sector preoccupation with procedures runs

deep. One non-profit agency operating a group home for the disabled, for example, must ensure the right number of calories per meal, the proper distance of a bed from a fire escape, and a certain number of hours of credentialed hands laid daily on a client. Few regulations speak to whether the person gets better. Input funding and input management can only be satisfied if we are comfortable with the equation that perfect service to customers is equivalent to perfect compliance with procedures. Resistance to that notion is at the heart of this book.

Our view is that governments must move from their intensive scrutiny of inputs to a focus on results. Our outcome approach offers a specific and practical set of tools by which the public sector can move from the role of funder to that of investor. In this framework, government agencies, like other investors, are concerned primarily with gaining a return.

In times of shrinking public sector budgets, outcome thinking moves from being important to being essential. On the one hand, there are simply no dollars to spend on ineffective activities. On the other, in many government agencies the only way to start a new program is to cease funding an old one. The investor approach can clearly identify those programs for which the return is low, or even non-existent. Effective investment hinges just as strongly on knowing when to stop as on when to start.

Finally, our approach holds a new view on an old adage. The cry for doing "more with less" is an admonition to government workers that is not only stale but disheartening. It is, however, an admonition very effectively applied to government's funds. Investments, whether in bridges or literacy, need to work as hard as do people.

As consultants to many governments, we have come to

appreciate the limited value of the realm called strategy. Strategic planning and direction often tells groups what they already know. Empower your workers. Engage total quality management. Provide the highest possible customer service. The critical need is not for new strategies. It is for tactics to implement the strategies we already have! This book intends to give you a practical approach for implementing an "outcome focus." At the same time, it relies on judgement and meaning, not facile charts and checklists.

Here is what we include to define and illustrate the Outcome Funding approach:

PART I profiles the way things are. We first review government's traditional mindset of funder, then analyze the conventional proposal and its elements. Proposal response--"grading the paper"--comes next, followed by considering the post-grant period. In all parts of the process, we identify key problems and their causes.

New to this edition, based on state, county, and city requests for our help, is a focus on budgeting. The translation is not difficult, in that budgeting reflects the inward application of funding. The same procedural focus is in evidence. More importantly, the shift from budgeting a department to investing in a department is just as timely. The principles are largely the same.

PART II outlines the Outcome Funding approach, beginning with a definition of the public investor. A project target plan is next defined as the core document for investor scrutiny, and its critical elements are explained. "Due Diligence" is then explained as an interactive methodology, in which the investor first verifies key representations made about projects, then makes investment decisions. The post-investment period is then discussed, with emphasis on how agencies support their investments to ensure that they yield a high return.

Budgeting reenters, with some specific tools defined for Outcome Funding application. Finally, for grantmaking or budgeting, we offer thoughts on getting started. Most of us know what we want to do. The question is how to do it. Points of resistance are mapped, along with strategies for surmounting them.

PART III looks in depth at targets and outcomes. We begin with the proposition that it is possible to specify clear and unequivocal performance targets for virtually all programs in which government invests, then to provide tools for doing so.

Milestones come next--those critical threshold points that signify that a project is on target in achieving its goals. Milestone management is presented as a distinctive practice. This chapter is largely new, reflecting such tools as the customer "funnel" and conversion ratios from one step to another that our clients have found very helpful.

We then turn to how best to confirm that targets are reached, suggesting that the conventional approach of evaluation is a red herring for many investors and implementors alike. The real point is verification, not measurement. Our final chapter in this section looks at a powerful tool for investor and implementor alike, called learning.

Part IV turns to the special case of innovation. Our premise is that investors who wish to prompt new solutions must use very different strategies from those who seek a direct return from existing practices. We begin with a look at those private sector innovators called entrepreneurs, and at the venture capital firms who seek and support them. A number of guidelines for public sector innovation investment are suggested by this framework. We then describe how investors can systematically enable innovative projects that can lead change by example. Funding change is very different from funding programs.

Notes in the book, located at the end of each section, go beyond references. They include additional musings and examples for readers interested in a particular point or premise.

While we focus on the public sector, the basic investment methodology is equally relevant to foundations, corporations, and individuals who distribute or allocate funds to achieve social ends. Although much less constrained, their practices have, in general, remained resistant to change. They, too, tend to hallow the proposal.

In any publication which forcefully suggests such a major change, the reader deserves a word on the approach of those who would persuade them. In our case, we provide you with two points. First, this book has its origin less in theory than in practice. In our work with the Innovation Group at The Rensselaerville Institute, we have been privileged to be partners with a wide variety of government groups in the United States, Canada, and the UK who have set aside "Request for Proposal" and picked up on the Outcome approach. We have learned through trying a great number of things and looking carefully at what works and what does not. Ours is, on balance, an empirically-based inquiry.

Second, we have a high regard for people in government service, and in groups who receive and expend their monies to achieve public purposes. Indeed, our contention is that the problems we identify are due not to people, but rather to the structures to which they are currently bound.

We are very grateful to our colleagues in The Innovation

Group—Valerie Chakedis, Thomas Gaines, David Hallowell, John LaRocca, Fredda Merzon, and Andrea Persico—for their impressive work in developing and applying the tools discussed in this book. We also thank Nancy Clickman, Anna Dickerson, and Kathleen Speck for their invaluable help with book production and outreach.

Finally, a strong measure of appreciation for the international perspective brought by Peter Mason and his UK colleagues in public and voluntary sectors. Peter is now launching a London-based Innovation Group (UK) and will offer Outcome Funding support there as well as a UK edition of the quarterly journal, *INNOVATING*. We are pleased that our concepts now spread far and wide.

Harold S. Williams
President, The Rensselaerville Institute
Rensselaerville, NY

Arthur Y. Webb
Chief Executive Officer,
Villages Centers of Care
New York City

William J. Phillips
Director, The Innovation Group
The Rensselaerville Institute
Rensselaerville, NY

September 1993

PART I:

The Way Things Are

One day, through the primeval wood
  A calf walked home as good calves should;
But made a trail all bent askew.
  A crooked trail as all calves do…

The trail was taken up the next day
  By a lone dog that passed that way;
And then a wise bell-wether sheep
  Pursued the trail o'er vale and steep,
And drew the flock behind him too
  As good bell-wethers always do.

And from that day o'er hill and glade
  Through those old woods a path was made.
And thus, before men were aware,
  A city's crowded thoroughfare…

A hundred thousand men were led
  By a calf near three centuries dead.
They followed still his crooked way
  And lost one hundred years each day.

Samuel Foss

Chapter 1

Government as Funder

When government agencies attempt to achieve their purposes through the efforts of others, their perceived role is most typically that of funder. This function focuses less on the consequences of funding and more on the act of giving out money.

Funding as a Mindset

The funding task is often underscored by other terms. One is resource allocation. Just as dollars are allocated within the organization, so too are they allocated beyond it. The function is distributional. Money is spread in an efficient manner over many needs and purposes which compete for attention.

Another concept is procurement. In many states, the selection of vendors to perform social and human services is set in the same "public bid" framework as the purchase of vans and newsprint. The requirement is to be a responsible purchaser. In procurement, price becomes predominant as the agency seeks the "lowest responsible bidder." Often, a number of firms are first qualified on a technical basis, with unit price then used to select vendors. This can refer to a contract for forty training hours just as readily as for forty portable computers. Gradations of quality are less important than variances in cost. [1]

Still another image which reinforces the funder perspective is that of "pass-through." Many public agencies spend money that others have given them to distribute. State agencies, for example, routinely receive and distribute Federal funds. Also, many funds—such as block grants—are structured to flow directly to a local level without specific knowledge of end use.[2]

Given that legislators are fond of believing that they solve problems by financial appropriations, it should not prove surprising that operating agencies often believe that they, in turn, meet needs by distributing such monies. From the perspective of both the appropriator and the funder, there is a tendency to believe that the program is the money.

As with many aspects of government which prevail over time, funding has become positioned in process terms. The "funding process"—like the budgeting process and the employee involvement process—falls victim to several fates common in process thinking. One is circularity. Consider the many diagrams and charts drawn by analysts to depict funding cycles. As one treatise puts it, "The ubiquitous arrows connote not only flow but a perverse form of self-sufficiency. In the tidy domain of process, the finish line always seems to circle back to the starting point."[3]

A problem stemming from the endless nature of processes is the difficulty in asking for outcomes. It is always possible to join the procedural march. It is much harder to step out of the parade to gauge just how far you have come, or when you will or should stop. Indeed, the process mindset asks us to focus not on outcomes but on activities. It is what we do that counts. In this case, the activity of government is funding.

Funding Functions

Just what does the funding process fund? Five functions are often present in a funding program:

l. Need. Government often supports those who make the best case that they are dealing with the greatest need. This needs focus justifies not only the funding program but the agency behind it. Where would the organization be if the need it was establishing to meet ever went away? The needs preoccupation takes many forms. The issuing of task force and commission reports, which highlight problems and seek a larger budget to deal with them, is one example. The RFP process with its emphasis on the needs statement is another.

From an Outcome perspective, the preoccupation with needs raises several concerns. First, the needs of clients may merge with the needs of helpers to create a misguided beacon for dollars.[4] Second, there can be a confusion between needs and desires. Legislative "member items" are justified on the premise that local residents "know what they need." Analysis of funding patterns suggests that residents are more likely to know what they want than what they need.

Two bigger problems prevail. One is that the funding of need becomes self-validating. As long as the dollars fall toward the depth of the problem, something useful is presumed to be happening. Government is doing the "right thing," but we do not know if it is doing things right. Second, "needs" are substituted for something far more important when outcomes are at stake: an understanding of the individuals who have that need.

2. Capacity. A quite different disposition is to fund the helpers rather than their clients. The point in this case is often the desire to have a group in place to operate a range of programs rather than to gauge likely performance on any given project. A government mandate to provide certain services—often in remote or difficult settings—is seen as jeopardized if the one group readily available to deliver such services is not kept alive. Capacity-building gains strength from its adjustment within the broad and honored public sector tradition. Government is fond of funding physical infrastructure—roads, industrial park sites, and the like—as a means to attract industry and better times. With groups which are funded to operate a variety of programs with public monies, capacity becomes organizational infrastructure.[5]

While just as logical as the needs focus, the capacity orientation also has its drawbacks. One is that assistance—especially to help a group get a grant in the first place—favors those most skillful and willing to adapt their proposals to the words and beliefs of the funder.

A second problem is that the perception of "no options" is seldom lost on supplicants, who quite rightly sense that the funder has become dependent on them. When no new groups are presumed possible or politically desirable, some settings can even take on the cast of a monopoly with respect to a vendor of publicly-funded services. Indeed, it is somewhat ironic that a government worried about free trade and anti-trust in the private sector is willing to grant implied franchises exclusive territories in its own sector.[6]

Finally, capacity itself becomes a form of input focus when we fail to hold it accountable for creating results. While others often speak of the broader goals of capacity building, we prefer to reverse the order. A specific capability is a means to an end.

3. Methodology. Simply put, the preferred approach becomes the funded approach. If a given environmental department believes that sewage lagoons outperform package treatment plans, that is what they will select and that is what supplicants will propose. If an agency believes that education is the key to employment, job training programs, and literacy development, that agency will gain the nod over early placement and on-the-job supports. In funding a given approach, the governmental unit is doing more than supporting projects presumed to work. It is ensuring the primacy of the method itself.

Methodology is seldom forged in a vacuum. In addition to the particular persuasions of those in power, for example, comes the factor of visibility. In many problem areas where outrage follows incident (child abuse, for example), the need is strong to be perceived as "doing something." Thus, the methodology of mass-media campaigns is a congenial fit between an approach that is presumed to help prevent a problem and one that, by its public visibility, reflects action at critical times. Our taxes are at work.

In order to fund methodology, one has to justify it. Thus, applicants are often advised to cite the theoretical basis for their project. This is particularly pronounced in education, where making something work in practice may prove easier than making it work in theory!

One drawback to the methodology approach is its "all-or-nothing" disposition. Rather than acknowledge that a given approach may work best for a given sub-population, the tendency is to become broadly prescriptive. Methodology funding does not generally support diversity. When the government funder goes beyond the specification of results to the specification of how best to achieve them, it is denying the applicant the right to prescribe what best fits a given situation. Also, a focus on methodological purity or consistency can deny implementors evolutionary growth and change.

4. Distribution. This objective is typically a matter of equity. Implicitly or explicitly, balances or even formulae are to be observed on such bases as demography (e.g., urban and rural), race, population, or problem incidence. At times, the issues are codified or at least connected to entitlements and rights. When politics enter the funding process, they generally enter in this realm. Legislators, for example, who support a given applicant are often less interested in the capacity or welfare of that group than in pulling dollars into their district. The distribution focus is as likely to land on the helpers as on those assisted. The interests of the vendor are often at issue more than the rights of those the vendor would serve.

5. Predictability. A key requirement in the public sector is to avoid unpredictable and adverse events. From the viewpoint of the funder, the worst thing that can happen is not tepid incompetence, but pungent screw-up. Indeed, leaders are often very clear that their key persons should, above all, keep their agencies out of the media with bad news. This admonishment strongly guides funders to stay clear of high-gain prospects if they are also high risk, and favors going with known commodities—whether agencies, methods, localities, or anything else.

Such an orientation also nicely circles back to the first focus—the needs orientation. Implementors who anchor to problems are more predictable than those who capture opportunities. Problems tend to be stable and durable, while opportunities can be volatile and short-lived.

In addition to the inherent limitations of these five funding approaches lies the problem of mixing and matching. When the orientations are put together, strengths can actually cancel out. For example, a funder interested in need and capacity may find that a given proposal scores very high in one dimension but very low in the other. The result is a lower average score than might be given to a program which scores just above average in all categories, but which is not outstanding in any dimension.

Funding Routine

If a venture capital firm used the same criteria to select entrepreneurs and business plans in 1990 that it used in 1950, it would be dead in a year. Yet government agencies continue to use precisely the same requests for proposals, and precisely the same funding questions and criteria through the years and even the decades. Apparently these funders have learned virtually nothing that enables them to change their own behavior to get higher returns for monies expended. This is actually logical and understandable given the focus on the funding act itself. So long as procedural compliance and internal criteria can be tightened without knowledge of outcomes, there is no reason to change the process to achieve higher returns. For funders to take on the same learning curve they wish to see evident in applicants, a new tool is needed.

Chapter 2

The Proposal

When government and non-profit groups funded by public monies think about either starting a new project or continuing an old one, they do so using the descriptive format known as **The Proposal**. Here is its template.

The Needs Statement. Profile the nature and depth of the problem in comprehensive terms. Show evidence of knowledge of all relevant data.

Goals and Objectives. Indicate the long-term goals and measurable objectives for your project.

Project Description. Describe the concept and the delivery mechanisms of the services you will provide. Describe your project in comprehensive terms.

Work Plan. Indicate in highly specific terms the phases and steps-within-phases that you will undertake to accomplish your objectives. Also include a management plan and Gantt chart.

Staffing Plan. Supply the job description of all key roles in the program. Include vitae of the persons to fill these positions or, if individuals are not yet identified, a complete job description.

Credentials of Proposing Group. Describe the past experiences of the applicant organization relevant to this project. Include a history of the organization and show evidence of its capability to handle the proposed project.

Evaluation Design. Show how you will measure all objectives. Include all relevant pre-tests and post-tests, as well as control groups.

Line Item Budget. Provide a complete line-item budget for the program. In personnel, indicate the percent of time that a staff person will work on the project and provide a justification for the purchase of any equipment.

Letters of Support. Include any letters of support from community-based groups, professional associations, and others with whom you have shared your proposal. Special consideration will be given to evidences of networking.

Applicants quite rightly assume that their proposal will be reviewed and graded. Great attention is paid to how words will be understood, with a general disposition to parrot back whenever possible the words of the RFP itself. The profession of grantwriter-specialist who helps applicants to compete effectively for government funds, attests to this pressure. Grant consultants are to non-profit organizations as college admission consultants are to high school students; they show them how best to take the test.

Regrettably, the exam can be murky. While the point system and reviewer criteria are crystal clear, the proposal architecture is not. Categories are often overlapping and are imprecise. For example, one RFP we reviewed had these directions in three distinct sections:

"Describe how the project is to be conducted to respond to the need identified..."

> "Elaborate the project's methodology..."
>
> "Define the work plan and critical assumptions linking elements together..."

While all of this—and much more—may sound good to the funder, it becomes a morass for respondents. They do not know where to put things. As a result, redundancy abounds and most proposals are twice as long as they need to be![7]

Beyond the inconveniences of time and expense to complete the grant application, what's the problem? A big one. The reality is that most and sometimes all of the content of the traditional proposal fails to address three critical questions which government as an investor should ask: 1) What results am I buying?; 2) What is the probability that I will get it?; and 3) Am I getting it at the least cost for the greatest gain?

The Proposal Dissected

Let's look, one by one, at the components of the typical proposal to see why it is remarkably unconnected to these questions.

The needs statement. What is the correlation between highly proficient, comprehensive, accurate, and correctly spelled needs statement, and the likelihood that a given project is clear on results and will work? The connection is from very weak to non-existent. There *is* a relationship between a proficient needs statement and the ability to use secondary data sources. There is an even stronger correlation between a quality needs statement and the presence of a grantwriter. But in most projects, government is less interested in buying research capability or funding employment than in gaining a result.

In reality, most projects brought to government departments for funding are not responding to a broad need at all. They are responding to specific individuals who have expressed that need.

Goals and objectives. Proposers here wax eloquent on the visions and values—not to mention purposes, missions, and beliefs—to which they are committed. They fail, however, to state in specific terms just what they are willing to be held accountable to achieve. When those fabled "measurable objectives" *are* stated, they often turn out to be inputs, not outcomes. The proposer indicates that it will develop at least four sixty-second television public service announcements on family abuse, or hold at least sixteen counseling sessions for at least forty-eight battered women. To what effect? At best, direction is clear, but the actual destination is not.

Project description. This section states what a group will do. It is discursive and comprehensive. Boundaries and limits are pushed back, and one good thing supposedly leads to another. The problem is that the funder is less concerned with the peripherals of the program than with its core. Most descriptions fail to define in concrete terms the product offered, let alone its comparative advantages over other products which purport to accomplish the same purpose.

Key descriptions include such terms as *process, system, and network.* Such labels provide the illusion of specificity more than reality. For example, a program which is described as a "process" gains the appearance of constant motion. Flows predominate, and content becomes much less important than structure and sequence. Systems and networks are fashionable because of their elasticity. They readily expand to imply all elements sought by the funder as well as the proposer.

Work plan. The presumption is that groups who have the most detailed idea of every step that they will undertake are most likely to be successful. Sophisticated grantwriters often suggest that there be at least four phases and at least five steps delineated within each phase in order to reflect careful thought.

The problem is one of timing. While people can glibly spin out a highly explicit forecast of steps they will take in advance of implementation, the reality is that once into their program for even a week, implementors know a number of elements that should be added to and subtracted from the work plan. Indeed, if an organization is held to dutifully implement only those steps that it can anticipate in advance, its project is almost surely doomed to failure.

A second problem concerns the "delivery schedule" often included here. It is generally more important to deliver the final report than to deliver a result worth reporting upon!

Staffing plan. This reflects the most critical shortfall in proposal logic. Roles and responsibilities of key people are delineated in precise detail. The presumption is that the structure is the key to effective implementation. As long as the right credentials and degrees are specified, persons needed to fill key slots are viewed as widely interchangeable. Hence, only a job description is needed for individuals.

In reality, the choice of specific individuals to lead implementation can be the most critical factor in ensuring success. As smart funders have discovered over and over, the right person can make even a weak plan work and a brilliant plan can be rendered impotent by uninspired implementors.

One reason the person is not "front and center" in many proposals is that the funder has signaled that this factor is unimportant. Here is a summary of the scoring for a grant application to fund training courses:

1. Understanding need (20 points maximum)
   a. Discuss grant application's requirements: 0 - 10 points
   b. Philosophical statement: 0 - 10 points

2. Addressing Need (50 points maximum)
   a. Work plan: 0 - 10 points
   b. Emergency room curriculum: 0 - 10 points
   c. Ambulance/law enforcement curriculum: 0 - 10 points
   d. Consultation description: 0 - 10 points
   e. Evaluation plan: 0 - 10 points

3. Qualification and Experience of Staff (30 points maximum)
   a. Organizational chart: 0 - 5 points
   b. Personnel practices and policies: 0 - 5 points
   c. Previous experience: 0 - 5 points
   d. Personnel: 0 - 5 points
   e. Supervision: 0 - 5 points
   f. References: 0 - 5 points

Total: 100 points maximum

We know that in training, as in other forms of education, the teacher is clearly the most critical variable. Yet here that person is worth five points—the same as his or her supervisor. Need, evaluation, and curriculum are all worth more.

If the individual is such a critical variable in effective programs, why has the public sector been so prone to avoiding this finding? We have two answers. First, government prefers collective to personal accountability. It is the procedure, the structure, or the system which can be found in error, but never an individual. Second, evaluators stress the importance of teamwork and tend to resist the proposition that it is the idiosyncratic person that can make a key difference. From a theoretical perspective, it would be much cleaner if we could have "lawful variables" which are predictable, understandable, and consistent.

Credentials of the proposing group. In focusing on the stability and continuity of an organization and on its past accomplishments, this section is useful but insufficient. It ignores the great variability *within* many organizations. If we are worried about a child's placement in a school system, we are assuredly concerned with the reputation of the district, the appearance of the particular building, and the outlook of the principal. But we are more concerned with the specific classroom in which our child will be placed. Virtually all schools have some teachers and programs that work extremely well and others that do not. Qualifications at an organizational level presume a uniformity that often does not exist.

A second problem is that credentials may be outdated. Just as some colleges and universities can live for a decade on a reputation no longer justified, so too can non-profit groups and others delivering government services.

Evaluation design. In this ubiquitous section, we learn of pre-tests and post-tests, and the ever-present questionnaires. If the applicant wants to cover all bases, the key prescription will be to hire an "outside evaluator" to take care of all of this. And reference to a "control group" never hurts! One problem with evaluation designs is that they are rarely understood or liked by program implementors or funders. Both can find them threatening, although for different reasons. The bigger problem is the presumption that comfort for the funder lies in project documentation in the first place. If the grantmaker waits until the end of the project to ask "What happened?" the opportunity to improve results comes too late.

Line-item budget. This is the only section of the proposal concerned with money. It is generally constructed with a literal focus on each line. The primary form of item integration is arithmetic. Do the numbers, once separately established, add up accurately and to a total within the limits of the program?

While the line-item approach allows for cost component scrutiny, it is not helpful in understanding the relationship of cost to benefit. We know the salary of the executive director, but not what value he or she will add to a given product.

When a cost benefit analysis is done, it compares inputs. Thus a funder can contrast proposals for a training program on the benchmark of "cost per training hour," but generally there is no way of relating cost unit to benefit unit. We know the cost of getting the training, but not the cost of getting to a result from and for those trained.

A plan for financial self-sufficiency is required in some proposal budget sections. It is designed to provide the funder with assurance that a program will continue after its support ends. Ironically, this is generally defined not as self-reliance in such terms as revenues generated, but as an ability to attract *other* outside funders to continue the program. We have seen instances where, in a given year, programs supported by a department of social services switched to support by a department of education, while an equal number of programs funded by education moved over to social services. This is an unusual form of self-sufficiency!

The notion of "leveraging" buttresses this process. An agency is generally concerned not with the total budget of the project, but with that proportion to which they contribute. If a funder believes that it is enabling a major program by adding a fraction of its total program cost, it is often happy indeed. From a taxpayer's perspective, however, the total picture is far more important than these increments and their shifts.[8]

Letters of support. Among the attachments in the typical proposal are testimonial statements such as, "We hope you will choose to support this most impressive program." Many are written by state legislators, mayors, heads of groups, and others who indicate no particular knowledge of the project to be undertaken. Even in those instances where the supporters are knowledgeable and specific, how could they be anything other than utterly laudatory? Like the tremendous inflation in letters of recommendation for colleges and other programs, letters of support must be unrelentingly positive to be deemed useful.

Summing up. The typical proposal is overstuffed but undernourished. It does not contain the information the funder needs to understand specifically what he/she is buying, the likelihood that he/she will get it, or the fairness of the price. Proposals are need-focused, paper-driven, constituent-weighted, activity-based, and anchored to the line item budget. Their power lies not in what they convey, but in what they are. Regrettably, the correlation between the high-scoring document and the high-performing project is often a weak one.

From the applicant's perspective, the drawbacks of the proposal are different but equally substantial. When an grant application is issued, it triggers the expenditure of often thousands of dollars of time by potential implementors. Indeed, this particular form of fund-raising can take as much as twenty-five percent or more of revenues generated.[9] The opportunity cost—time taken from serving people—is enormous. Ironically, funders will often speak proudly of proposal rounds that attract hundreds of applications for a small number of grants. From their perspective, this popularity gives added value. But from the perspective of public services, the inefficiencies overwhelm the gains.

Equally important, the time expended in completing the proposal by the supplicant is a sunken cost. In most instances, it cannot be recovered even if the project is funded. What is done to get money is unconnected to what is done to spend it. Fine-tuning the proposal format is of little use. A new approach is needed.

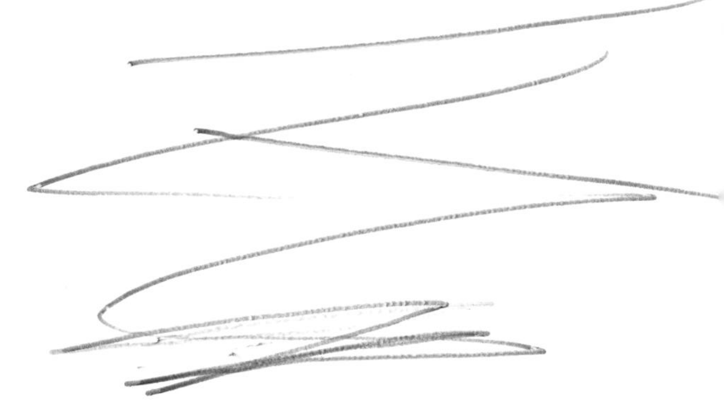

Chapter 3

Grading the Paper

While calls for proposals generate a flurry of dispersed applicant activity, the due date triggers an equal but concentrated effort by the funder. Proposals are logged in, duplicated, statistically profiled, and distributed for initial review. A complicated and multi-faceted process unfolds, documented and tracked by Gantt charts and a variety of instruments and checklists. The work is earnest and hard and, generally, efficient. This is government at its best, or, at least, at its busiest.

The process is well-established. After an initial completeness check, proposals go into some sequence of reviews, often a combination of individual study and group scrutiny. Some reviewers are funding agency staff, while others come from a variety of external roles, such as content expert, evaluator, and those who represent "community-based" viewpoints. The only persons generally conspicuous by their absence are customers for the programs proposed.

The core business is grading the paper. Points are awarded for each proposal section. Scores are then correlated with the monies available to determine the cut-off point. For a proposal not funded, the response is clear: "Sorry. You scored an eighty-four and you needed at least a ninety to be funded." Numerical scores are deemed comprehensive and comparable. It is much more soothing to tell someone his/her number was too low than to say, "Your proposal was not funded because Joe and Nancy did not believe the person designated to run it could pull off the stated results."

Behind the scoring is a mechanistic framework in which equity is presumed. The impartiality inherent in adding, weighing, averaging, and comparing points is a broad shield. It reassures not only applicants but funders as well. If a selected project later fails, there is no one person to blame. Such diffusion of responsibility, of course, is a characteristic not only of government but of many large organizations.

Key Characteristics of Proposal Review

This conventional review approach has a number of features. Here are ten, annotated with the problems they bring. While not each characteristic is present in every selection process, together they reflect the generic philosophy and practice of the proposal review.

1. *Business at Arm's Length.* The review process purposely isolates reviewers from applicants. Rarely is personal interaction permitted. Rather, when questions arise, inferences are drawn from the proposal. Review groups may spend inordinate time trying to decide what a proposal author meant by a given sentence or word.

Distance as a sanitizing factor is seen as ensuring equity. All proposers are treated fairly by being treated exactly the same. And certainly the notion of a contest brings ample precedent of isolating the judges from the contestants.

Another form of equity—doing whatever it might take to ensure that each proposal is well understood by its own terms—is foregone. As a result, when reviewers do meet proposers after the selection process is complete, they often find that many of their inferences are inaccurate.[10] This could have been prevented with a five-minute phone call.

2. *Freezing the Action.* Once submitted, most proposal reviews do not allow for change. The selection process

is reactive to and dependent upon the submission. Ironically, many changes will be allowed following selection, as circumstances and needs change during a project. While reviewers may spot at least some of these matters, no interactive process to anticipate and to mitigate them is permitted.

Think of the lost potential. Seasoned and bright persons have devoted hours to looking critically at a given project. At the end of their review, many have highly useful insights into how a project could be made stronger, whether funded in this particular instance or not. Project leaders are not likely to have the budget or inclination to assemble as much insight during the entire course of their project!

Sadly, there is no process either during or after the review to harness reviewer thinking for project improvement. Instead, applicants must ask for a review summary under Freedom of Information legislation, in what is seen by both sides as a defense of decisions made. Thus, in still another way, the selection of projects is disconnected from implementation.

3. *"Points Off" for Shortcomings*. While often implicit, the premise of many reviews is that proposals begin with a perfect score and accrue negative points for what is deficient. Reviewers are provisioned with checklists, and if something is missing, the score is reduced. While on the surface both egalitarian and positive, this approach is actually negative. It focuses on weaknesses, not strengths. The presumption is that a project with no discernible shortcomings is of higher quality than one with some drawbacks or omissions but an outstanding core strength.

Worse, grantwriters are adept at making sure that all bases are covered rhetorically, which is where it counts. Their agility is aided by the RFP itself, which generally highlights or at least alludes to the important things to say. Proposal writing is marketing and, in this case, the funder makes it clear what is needed. The request for proposals and the responding documents are in a partnership that is remarkably self-contained.

4. *"Points On" for Consistency.* One way to understand how closely the grant application process approximates a closed system is to look at the focus on internal consistency. Reviewers are trained to spot points at which proposal sections prove contradictory or in other ways fail to add up to a congruent presentation. If a group says they will hold fourteen workshops for ten people in one place and speaks of "the 120 persons to be served" in another, skepticism is justified and a high grade for the paper is unlikely.

Congruence of the proposed project to its own surroundings or to other external factors is far less important. Further, external factors are not readily understood. Rarely is there the time or place in the review process to verify the representations made about customers, problems, opportunities, etc.

5. *Decision by Plurality.* An impressively large number of persons can be involved with each proposal. Here is one profile:

Function	Number of Persons
Initial completeness review	1
Internal review panel	3
Expert reviewers	2
Community-based panel	6
Evaluation consultant	1
Final selection	2
	15

Assuredly, the inclusion of more people in the review process is presumed to be functional. It provides widespread involvement by interests which might otherwise feel excluded. It creates an internal industry of reviewers within agencies that justifies staff positions and exercises control. It lowers the effect of any one individual. For these purposes, the more collective the process, the better.

For purposes of a smart decision, however, fewer people may be far better than more. At the very least, the "value added" question should be raised. What is the effect on the quality of grant decisions if ten people touch the proposal instead of fifteen? And what is the loss if it drops to five? Indeed, private-sector experience suggests that we inquire not only into the prospect of loss from reduced numbers but of gain as well! Groups have a tendency to reduce decisions to common denominators and to filter out provocative proposals with sharp edges.

Another concern with the high numbers of reviewers is cost. When the expense of all review time is "loaded" onto those proposals that are funded, we have found that for smaller grants *the cost of selection can exceed the cost of the grant!*[11]

6. *The Summary as the Glue.* The review process is like a relay race, with each person handing the baton to the next. At most points, it is not the proposal that is handed on but rather a distillation of its content. The nature of the proposal becomes less critical than the nature of its summary—and what the synthesizer chose to include and exclude.

This reductionist strategy is seen as necessary. Large numbers of people and proposals must narrow to a reasonable decision canvas. The drawback, however, is that those persons who make the final decisions are actually relying on the thinnest of data bases. With summaries, the tendency is to move toward broader statements that define projects in categorical terms. In final discussions, you hear such thoughts as:

- Which of these proposals is most community-based?
- Is that the one that proposes teacher involvement?
- Let's focus on those that are realistic.

Essential points of understanding and discrimination are lost. Indeed, those proposals that do not readily fit within broad categories will not fare as well as those which do.[12]

7. *The Reviewer Agendas.* Reviewers invariably bring their own ideas to the proposal. In application response, where you stand can be determined by where you sit. Here are some forms in which that philosophy plays out:

- *Back-scratching.* Certain people whose proposals are reviewed may soon sit in judgment of the reviewer's own submission. Reciprocity is never far from the mind.

- *Feasibility judgment.* A reviewer may well deem something not feasible because he/she tried it and failed...or saw others do so. Deciding what is "realistic" is generally a personal matter.

- *Theoretical resonance.* Many experts favor one theory over another, and let points follow preference. They can also lower points for a program with no stated theory—regardless of the quality of the proposed practice.

- *Place legitimacy.* Community-based input often centers around whether the proposer has lived in or understands the community. While the nature and boundaries of the community in question may be murky, this perspective can be strongly influential.

8. *Staff Advocacy and Protection.* Agency staff who review proposals rarely come with a blank slate. In many instances, they know the proposers from past contracts. This experience becomes the filter by which each new proposal is reviewed. One indicator is the extent to which a staff person can become first an advocate and then a protector of favored programs. "I realize there are some minor deficiencies in the proposal, but I know this group; believe me, they are good." Alternatively, one or more bad experiences will similarly color the current proposal and its grade.

In either event, there is a regrettable confusion—both between past and present and between an organization and its various programs. Generalizations tend to ignore variability. Also, the reason a person likes or dislikes an applicant may have nothing to with the funding criteria.
Advocacy tilts the playing field. In particular, new groups face an incline. They have not yet established a protector or an experience rating. They are a bit like first-time credit applicants. There is no borrowing history to reassure the financier.

9. *Viewpoint Weighing*. Input on proposals come from staff, evaluators, external experts, community-based persons, etc., and is weighed in as a factor in the final decision. Typically, there is no integration or synthesis perspectives. Rather, different opinions and judgments are connected numerically.

Perhaps the starkest separation is seen in two functions not only separable but often at odds. On the one side is the program shop, whose occupants often see themselves as sensitive to those with needs and those funded to deal with them. On the other side are contracts people—budget analysts, lawyers, etc.—who pride themselves on taking a hard look at what is to be delivered. Each side believes it is saving the agency from the excesses of the other. Separation becomes dichotomy. One consequence is that proposers are encouraged to respond to disparate interests in the review process by adding language to cover each area.

10. *Reliability as Quality Control.* If the proposal review system does not reward imagination in supplicants, it certainly awards predictability in reviewers. Regularity takes the form of reliability, a condition in which different individuals focusing on the same subject and using the same tools draw the same conclusions. The assured good is to have the checklists and frameworks so explicit and instrumented that different reviewers would come to the same rating of a given proposal even if operating independently. When this happens, a key criterion of quality control is presumed to be met. The process is then impersonal by definition; reviewers are interchangeable.

This goal is seldom reached. One reviewer's "12" for a work plan is another reviewer's "15." When points are added, this kind of unplanned and unseen variation can make the difference between funding and not funding. While the presumed value becomes illusive, an adverse side effect is consistently present.

Reversing the Practice

The collective drawbacks of proposal grading are serious. It is not only extensive and expensive, but misguided as well. The point is not to grade the proposal, but use it to understand the project it portrays. The paper grading process is complex and even tortuous in structure, but simple in judgment. We need a process that reverses that logic—a simple structure in which complex judgments can be accommodated.

Chapter 4

After the Grant

For both funder and grantee, the first thing recognized about the typical post-selection period is that it is anti-climactic. The peak experience is decision-making. At the funding agency, the recommendations have been made and sent "upstairs," often with legislators standing by to carry the good news to groups in their district. The organization is recognized for getting appropriated money out its door in a responsible way. Now it's on to the next grant cycle.

Over in the winner's circle, letdown is likely. When the announcement is received, the group is ecstatic. More money has been pulled into the agency to continue its important work. The top talent can now move to the next grant opportunity as the newly-funded project moves to line staff for implementation. For both sides, there is higher status in the act of giving and getting than in spending and supporting over the long haul.

Contracting

The main event following the grant announcement is not implementation. It is contracting. This is sufficiently important so that in many public agencies the entire grantmaking process is called "contract management." This step begins with development of a lengthy document containing both standard provisions and assurances and the specifics of this program. These features of the contracting process deserve mention, along with the problems they create.

The contracting process is prolonged. Indeed, it can take

longer than selection, leading to a time lag of up to one year between proposal submission and final contract. Time is further extended by review and approval of contracts by multiple "control" agencies. Picture the enthusiastic project director who can't wait to get started and has identified several time-bound opportunities. As the days, weeks, and then months go by, that enthusiasm is bound to wane. And in more than an occasional case, the time lag requires a switch of key persons; the original leaders now have something else to do.

Change

Remarkably, the same proposal which was considered immutable during its day of judgment can now be altered! Program and technical people will often work to refine the project such that it is "do-able." Indeed, the kinds of highly-productive interactions with implementors which are disallowed in the selection process can now enter, often sparked by lawyers who have had no role in selection. As a result, the final scope of work may be significantly different from the proposal in both content and quantity. Why does a system which can be so rigid during review become so loose when the real program is defined in contractual terms? Fairness issues are rightfully raised by this question.

Budget and Work Plan Focus

Beyond standard clauses and assurances, the primary point of control in the contract is financial. Budgets are now made part of the official document, as are payment dates and amounts. Allowable costs are tightly specified and flexibility to change amounts between budget categories is constrained.

The work plan is also included, occasionally tied to payment points. To get the second quarterly payment, the activities specified for the first quarter must be completed, or there must be an explanation. Notice that results are not in this picture. Indeed, budget and work plan discussions generally take place in the *absence* of any framework which ties these elements to outcomes.

Contract Monitoring

When the contract is executed, the project is launched. At this point, government-as-funder assumes the role of "monitor." Work is often limited to review of periodic reports which speak to completed activities, progress on meeting objectives, and barriers encountered. In most cases, the "narrative" information provided is highly general, and is reviewed to ensure completeness rather than usefulness of responses. What is monitored is not the project but its paper.[13] When monitors see a problem, red flags are waved and the agency works to bring the project into compliance.

The relationship formed by this perspective is a contingent one. It kicks in only when problems arise. There is no expectation that the funder will work to identify early warning signals, to add insight at strategic points, or to join in learning from the experience to make future projects better. Involvement is intended to remediate deficiencies, not to optimize achievement. The lack of relationship is abetted by the frequent transfer of responsibility from those who selected the project to those who will monitor it. As a result, the convictions or even the passion which led someone to back a project are unavailable to ensure its success.

Also, there is no sense of reciprocity. While the implementor promises deliverables to government, government in turn is not asked to provide any assurances to the implementor, whether on prompt payment or anything else. Simply put, funding alone does not trigger a partnership. Assuredly, many implementors welcome this approach: "Just give us the money and stay out of our hair." In general, grantees get their wish...and their projects are the lesser for disconnection to the one external agent which has the most stake in their success.

If implementors are burdened by the contracts process, they gain one blessing of great value. The tenet is clear that the organization has been awarded the full amount of the grant. Progress payments will be forthcoming unless there is a major transgression that would cause the program to be "defunded." That word says it all. The total funds are an entitlement. In this framework, results have a hard time in being consequential.

From grant application to proposal, from review to the post-selection process, the traditional funding approach of the public sector is a process nicely tuned to its constituents. It has safeguards against fraud, strong evidence of procedural accountability, rationality born in impersonal formulae, and widespread participation. All it lacks are results. Ways to identify, promote, and verify changes and benefits for program customers are simply not present. We now turn to the inward application of funding in organizations, where the same problems prevail.

Chapter 5

Funding Budgets

Our view of budgeting as now practiced in most governmental agencies is that it mirrors the funding process described in the above chapters. The only major difference is that fund recipients are internal and not external. The primary focus is on distribution of monies such that resource allocation is deemed fair, comprehensive, and responsible. Elaborate systems are used to first develop, then review and revise budget submissions during these halcyon days known as the budget season. The point of this process is to be fiscally sound. Indeed, budget agencies are called control agencies. They are designed to keep a sharp eye on the money. But they are not designed to ensure its optimal impact.

Budget as Process

Budgeting has a long honored set of traditions that includes many forms of gamesmanship. Agency leaders will often encourage a volume increase on the High Need in their area of public stewardship. Some are also known to deluge budget analysts with huge amounts of data designed to obscure points at which they are vulnerable. Part of the challenge, of course is to start high, knowing that negotiations and compromise will follow.

Behind the game, of course, lies the scorecard. The "budget winners" are those who get more money against the yardstick of the previous year or who do well relative to other parts of the system. An organization that has found ways to save money and therefore need less of it goes by a different name: a loser.

The budgeting cycle, like the grant cycle, tends to be viewed as an end in itself. The heavy work lies in allocating the money; spending it is anticlimactic. This is true not only for those who approve budgets but for those who submit them from operating units. Rarely is a budget used as a management tool during the year it is in effect. Assuredly, totals are remembered such that we spend responsibly—defined as within budget limits. But the power of budgets to guide performance through monthly comparisons of budget vs. actual expenses is seldom realized. At any given time, far more people are concerned with shaping next year's budget than using this year's budget as a roadmap. As with proposals, the document used to get money does not prove useful or vital in spending it.

The procedural focus is also reflected in the pursuits and aspirations of budget-makers who are largely preoccupied in these times with achieving the goal of the balanced budget. As necessary, revenue projections are inflated and expenses are deflated—often into bond and trust funds whose later cost is masked from next year's expenses. All told, more attention is placed on the balanced budget than on the effective budget. This may be the supreme (and certainly most legitimized) form of procedural ends outwitting outcomes.

Budgeting is big business. Budget analysts, managers, and overseers create and consume a major part of public sector overhead. But the true costs lie in the time of the budget seeker. Many persons in larger governmental systems and agencies indicate that budgeting takes a great deal of their time—as much as 10-15% on an annualized basis. Budgeting can stretch for weeks, as budget overseers call for new and different scenarios. As with grants, the scrutiny awarded a small allocation may be larger than the amount under the looking glass.

Budgeting is also a long business. Preparations begin at the operating level approximately 6 to 8 months before a budget is passed. Structurally, it is difficult to have budgets that are responsive to current conditions. Another duration factor is the overlap of budget cycles. It is not uncommon for units of government to be focused on either two or three budget years at all times. The complexity is overwhelming—and one reason budgeting is so costly.

The Two Sides of Budgeting

Budgeting has two primary components: building and brokering. At the micro level comes the preparation and subsequent analysis of budgets. The budget-builder seeks two ends for their financial edifice. One is the largest possible size, and the other is inclusion of favored items such as computer equipment. Even with so-called zero-based budgeting in which submitters are asked to start from scratch, the preparer works within severe limits. In many school districts and social and human service agencies, state and federal mandates comprise as much as 80% of all expenses. Budgeting is not a free-fall event, especially when the goal of avoiding layoffs is added. Attention is often focused on a narrow band of expenses.

Budget building includes review, where analysts are constrained and even conditioned by what they get. Reviewers look carefully at the reasonableness of costs and of cost departures from previous years. They also look at costs as appropriate to units of service or activity to be provided. If they do not also consider cost relative to units of achievement, they can be forgiven. The data now before them does not allow for this.

Analysts are the keeper of the efficiency flame. Theirs is a mission bent on justifying all costs expressed in a line item text. Categories are neatly separated. Educational administrators turn one day to instructional costs and the next to transportation. The result is an ironic juxtaposition of program efforts to integrate services contrasted with a financial model that clings to component thinking. Governments now seek to be "seamless" to their customers, who are presumed uninterested in divisions among departments, bureaus, and subjects. The separation between line items on the budget, however, remains firmly in place.

The second budgeting component shifts from micro to macro level, where a brokering process ensues. In some systems, this balancing and accommodating process is driven by rating and ranking systems which appear fully objective, if not scientific. They often separate essential items from "betterments" and take on the same general templates as the proposed review formats discussed in Chapter 3.

Whether quantified or not, degree of urgent need is also a factor, as is the requirement of appearing to be actively doing something about such critical problems as drug abuse and crime. The more blatant political acts, largely based on the needs of legislators for re-election in their district, are now largely separated into separate funding windows.

Most budgeting processes tend to include surprisingly little interaction between building and brokering. Once operating units have given them their "best shot" they generally surrender their proposed budgets to their agency heads. A similar hand-off occurs to budget departments and organizational leadership above the departmental level. The considerations that finally shape most budgets are different from the considerations that, often painstakingly, went into base formulations. Final budgets are often very different from submitted budgets, which often fail to convey any set of logic meaningful to the original preparer. This condition has a sad consequence: that people are often demoralized, getting a profound reminder of their lack of empowerment.

Very few people at operating levels truly own their own budgets.

The Meaning of Money

What budget seekers and makers, analysts and brokers miss in their respective preoccupations is how firmly the die is cast by the framework in which their roles play out. Budgets have their source in both legislative and executive leaderships and thus structurally disconnect the source of money from the accomplishments it is to enable. Indeed, source of money is the primary explanation of the differences between public and private sector organizations. Consider this set of distinctions:

Budget Based:	**Sales Based:**
Expands budget	Lowers cost
Satisfies funding sources	Satisfies customers
Rewards seniority	Rewards performance
Transmits value	Adds value
Emphasizes procedures	Emphasizes results

The concept of value-adding illustrates the difference. In a private sector company, whenever expense is added, there must be a corresponding added value that the customer sees and for which they are willing to pay. If having five persons review a memo does not improve its quality over having one person do so, the private sector cannot afford the added cost. Government, however, can readily budget for more people since the discipline of value-adding has bowed to the process of value transmission, where any number of people can get in the loop, often justified by a goal of participation.

Peter Drucker nicely summarizes the budget-based disconnect between money and its accomplishments:

“First, the public-service institution is based on a "budget" rather than being paid out of its results. It is paid for its efforts and out of funds somebody else has earned, whether the taxpayer, the donors of a charitable organization, or the company for which a personnel department or marketing services staff work. The more efforts the pubic-service institution engages in, the greater its budget will be. And "success" in the public-service institution is defined by getting a larger budget rather than obtaining results." [14]

NOTES, PART I

1. Ironically, many of the procedures in governments established to prevent fraud and "protect the taxpayer" have the effect of raising rather than lowering costs. Procurement agents in many states suggest that costs for many items—from pencils to buildings—can be 10-30% higher for government than when purchased in the private sector. A primary reason is the forms and processes of procedural accountability.

2. A more subtle form of the block grant is the program grant to a large agency that uses the money to support a variety of efforts, often in different locations. In most instances, only aggregate data is reported to the funder. In reality, the true investment is done by the agency which finances many individual projects within its own auspice.

3. Williams, Harold S. , "The Process Vs. The Product," ***INNOVATING***, Vol. 1, No. 1, 1990.

4. Foundations as well as government agencies can make follow-on grants based not on the success of implementors but on their failure. Support and interest often follow need, perhaps in part because funders literally go where they are needed.

5. The infrastructure focus for many programs strikes us as misguided. Whether building a road or an organization, the premise is that if you have the right foundation, development (whether economic or social) will follow. But, life is neither that simple nor that passive. In economic development, many impressive groups have shown that jobs in remote areas are more effectively created by importing

result-driven entrepreneurs than by improving facilities and waiting for the world to come to them. This same distinction may be present for organizational infrastructure.

6. Education is one area in which franchises are clear, which is why some reformers advocate a voucher system to create choice for consumers in public schools. Many non-profit organizations also have at least implied exclusive territory. Associations for Retarded Persons (ARCs), for example, may be the acknowledged sole provider of certain services for the disabled within a county.

7. The real problem with componentized thinking is that nothing is ever integrated. A number of "pieces" are allowed and encouraged to exist side by side—first on paper and then in reality. It is ironic that so many proposals proclaiming the wisdom of coordinated services are themselves, strongly fragmented.

8. A different kind of example comes from those funds used to acquire a resource that is then lost to its previous home. What is the net value of helping Harvard acquire a professor now teaching at Yale?

9. Assume a non-profit group responds to ten grant application requests in a year and is a winner in two instances for grants totalling $100,000. Further assume that the cost in time and direct expense for each proposal is $3,000. The $30,000 of cost to pull in monies thus reflects 30% of all monies raised. To keep this in perspective, most forms of fund-raising by non-profit groups are equally high if not higher in cost. Direct mail solicitations and award dinners, for examples, tend to have costs that are as high as 50% of all the revenues they raise.

10. Nothing is more striking than watching grantmakers meet their grantees for the first time! We invariably find that in some 10 to 30% of cases, the selector finds some notable discrepancy between who and what they had assumed they were funding and what they see and hear before them.

11. While government agencies rarely have available a cost-accounting tool which tells them how much they are spending on a given function, our occasional analyses suggest that review costs of $3,000 per proposal are not uncommon, especially when overhead is added to time. If 25% of all applications revised from $3,000 each are selected, the cost per funded project rises to $12,000. If 10% are funded, the cost per winner is $30,000.

12. Sophisticated grants-writers understand this process and purposely limit complexity. They not only do not wish to overreach the intellectual capacity of reviewers but want to make it easy to reduce the proposal to a specified category or type known to be favored in reviews. This is one reason in social programs that simplistic answers can chase complex problems.

13. An MIT professor known to us once submitted large sections of *Alice in Wonderland* in his quarterly reports to a federal government agency. In four years of such practice, not one comment other than "Good report" was received in return. Reviewer scans often stop with ensuring that all questions have been answered.

14. Drucker, Peter F., *Innovation and Entrepreneurship*, New York: Harper and Row, 1985, p. 179. As noted in the discussion of grant funding, government fails

to cost-account, its major central functions. As a result, public agencies can blithely continue their budgeting ways, secure in the wisdom that they are protecting the taxpayers' money. One study in Kentucky found that an agency budget of approximately $5 million cost about $600,000 to develop and approve—including all time and share of organizational overhead for everyone involved.

PART II:

The Outcome Alternative

God forgives those who invent what they need.

Lillian Hellman

Chapter 6

Government as Investor

When government views itself as a funder, it is primarily concerned with distributing money. When it sees itself as an investor, it becomes more focused on what happens after the grant. Funding remains a useful and accurate description when applied to the appropriation and supply of monies. Thus, legislative and executive budgets fund programs to respond to the homeless, drug abuse, and many other problems. The concept of investment enters as one or more agencies charged with dealing with a given problem employ funds to target investments to achieve specific benefits. This progression from funding to investing is the starting point for results.

The Idea of Investment Return

Investors seek a return. In the private sector, ROI (return on investment) is a relationship between the dollars which go into an enterprise and the revenues that come out. The dollars invested must do more than simply be preserved. They must create a return through their use.

The investor mode in government actually starts in the same place: money. Thomas Miller has advanced the concept of ROTI (return on taxpayers' investment). His emerging case study of a group called Kentucky Highlands Investment Corporation (KHIC) makes the point nicely.[15] KHIC receives central government monies and uses them to create jobs in Appalachian Kentucky. Its strategy is to invest in entrepreneurs and in small business expansions. The starting point for determining ROTI begins with the presumption that government's money is an investment seeking cash preservation and return. The true cost of the investment is readily computed by looking at the federal government's cost of borrowing money and then adding both the direct costs and overhead needed by the funding agency to select this group and to track the grant.

The return on investment begins at the direct level of the enterprises in which KHIC has invested. In brief, are they able to return the funds invested by KHIC? If so, the government has preserved its capital, although it is left it in place at KHIC through more investments. The analysis then goes further. For every job created, the following gains can be qualified as additional returns to the government: 1) reduction in public assistance and unemployment for people hired; 2) gain from income and payroll taxes, again from all people employed; and 3) reduced Medicaid and other health costs for health plans covered by employees. While these gains are generally labeled as "savings" to government, they can be considered returns which are directly created by governmental investment in KHIC. All told, these "revenues" created by the investment form the ROTI for the KHIC grants.

While few government investors carry investment logic to this end, there are many advantages in doing so. One is to justify grants in the first place. With rising deficits at both federal and state levels, the issue is no longer competition among agencies for funds to expend. The problem is justifying any expenditure at all. The notion of return separates those programs which become "sunken costs" from those where public money comes back in some form. While government may not get—or even want—its money back, the point is to know whether the investment is preserved, in order to keep producing. For this to happen, the capital must always be present and at work rather than expended and lost.

A second advantage of the return on investment concept is the cost control motivation it introduces. If a program costing $200,000 yields a 20% return in the form of economic or human gain, the ROTI literally doubles to 40% if the cost is only $100,000. Indeed, return is as influenced by the reduction in cost as by increase in outcome!

The final advantage is comparison. The investor has the ability to compare the return of a given project with that of other projects which might use a similar or different approach to create a benefit. Comparison is also valuable because it leads to learning. Just as stock investors pore over the past performance of the companies in which they invest, so too can the public investor. Did the anticipated returns emerge? If not, why not? In retrospect, was a better investment choice possible? If so, what factor was ignored that would have led to picking that alternative? The questions are pointed, and the answers shape future behavior.
All of this said, caution is still advised. It is neither possible nor helpful to attempt to reduce performance in many government-financed programs to a single "bottom line." There are often multiple forms of gains. Also, the assumptions underlying calculations—even in business—are as critical to understanding as are accounting methods. The point of investment return logic is less to sharpen the pencil than to sharpen the thinking.

In considering the concept of government as investor, care must be taken to keep it rigorous. The common rhetorical notions of "investing in the future" or "investing in children" fail to connect an act to a consequence in any direct way. Investment does not happen metaphorically.[16]

The Portfolio

Beyond the concept of return, the investor notion introduces the useful concept of portfolio and portfolio balance. Investors generally seek diversity, rarely putting all their eggs in one basket, no matter how enticing the basket. The same principle holds for the government agency that wishes to invest in social gains. Balancing may well be sought in such terms as:

Breadth and depth. Some programs load up resources intensively on a few people or settings. Others spread them out, so that a larger group of people can be touched by benefits and impacts. Interests of equity, visibility, and effectiveness suggest different approaches, as do assumptions about the minimal level of program intensity needed to achieve a given result. In some programs, the ideal cost might be $100,000 per person, while in another it may be $5. Note that this is a distinction of level of intensity, not level of grant amount. A small grant can be just as intensive as a large one.

Financing service and financing change. Some investments are designed to continue proven methods. The investors' assumption is that they know what needs doing and need only support it at an appropriate level. Other investments generate tests of new approaches and divergent thinking. To the extent that different problems need either current or new solutions, both kinds of investments may be needed.

Big programs and small programs. On the one hand, larger and more comprehensive programs can be an effective way to give out money. There are fewer choices to make and fewer groups to track. On the other hand, smaller groups often have lower overhead and can be more cost-efficient and responsive. The same amount of money can mean more to them, but the results are much less predictable. Again, a balance is needed.[17]

Established and new providers. Well-known implementors have that all-important "proven track record," but without a yardstick for new groups, the track can become a rut. A funding portfolio may need to contain both elements.

Ameliorating symptoms and attacking causes. Some programs deal with immediate and urgent conditions—providing shelter, food, and medicine, for example, where none is at hand. Others look to change the factors causing such needs. Both are often needed.

Funding study/funding action. In some areas, additional research might seem critical to inform enlightened programs. In others, more than enough studies already exist, and the need is to go from analysis to action.

Levels of risk. In many portfolios, a generally conservative stance is likely to be offset by a few longshots. The real trade-off in government is not between risk and reward, but between risk and predictability. Government can handle low or even no gain from a project much more readily than it can handle the unexpected outcome that draws taxpayer ire.

In general, the investors' balance of objectives should not only be explicit, but determined in advance of a funding cycle. This enables implementor energies to focus in those places where investors most want to go.

Investor Clarity

The effective investor is clear not only on portfolio balance, but on a number of "givens" for each investment round. These may include cost thresholds for a specific service or result, and methodologies favored or not favored. They will assuredly include the outcomes to which project results should and must contribute. (This critical point is covered in detail in Chapter 12.) Investing is not a game in which the financing agent is testing respondents to see if they know the right answers. Nor is it a fishing trip in which useful guidelines will be pulled from the process downstream. Outcome Funding begins with a high degree of investor clarity, which is then clearly shared. The mechanics are as straightforward as possible at all points.[18]

While there is currently openness in the proposal format, it goes in the wrong direction. Ten points awarded to the needs statement and twenty to the work plan is clarity applied to the proposal, not to the project! The point of explicitness on project givens is to ensure that the right information is present and also reduce the number of applications received. Investors who have not been totally and brutally clear on what they want, and then receive a great number of inappropriate applications, have caused unwarranted effort on the part of both supplicants and themselves. It is far more cost-effective (and remember that reducing costs is as important as increasing benefits in gauging return) to limit solicitations to those well-fitted to investor purposes.

The particulars in terms of results rather than activities are priorities that must begin with investors. If investors do not model this behavior, why should the respondents follow suit? At the least, investors preparing to spend money should either have a clear answer to these questions or delay the financing announcement until they do:

- What outcomes do we seek, and what range of performance targets for projects in which we invest do we specify?

- What are our portfolio objectives, and what is the rationale for each?

- What minimal overall return on investment do we seek in terms of tangible public gain?

- What is non-negotiable in terms of what implementors should or should not do in any area—methodology, geography, etc.?

- What do we most want to learn from our experience in this round of investments?

At first glance, such clarity may seem an inhibiting factor for implementors. In reality, it is an enabling one. When the investor is clear on "givens," it is a way of defining what is not given as well. Specifying boundaries and ends gives great latitude to implementors on both means and achievements they believe are connected to those ends. At present, lack of clarity and seemingly random forays into prescription make applicants reluctant to be assertive in any dimension.

Joint Investments

Just as banks and other institutional investors often go together to finance a project, so too are government funders increasingly inclined to joint venture projects. There are some good reasons for doing so. One is to get to a critical financing scale which is simply not possible for any one investor. A second is to reduce risks by spreading out. A third is the increase in both cost and program effectiveness that can be enabled when investors join forces.

In any given state, five or more separate agencies now deal with problems such as teen pregnancy, drug addiction, or housing. Redundant funding mechanisms abound as each agency duplicates the review process machinery of other agencies. From the implementor viewpoint, different regulations and reporting requirements from each agency are a nightmare. At best, they take precious time from implementation. At worst, they set up roadblocks and contradictions: what is legal and even encouraged in one program can be illegal or discouraged in another.[19] Coordinated investments can expose and correct such contradictions while consolidating redundant systems.

There are two ways to consolidate funds. One is to do so initially, so that groups combine and announce one pool of available monies. The other way is on a project-by-project basis. Funders in the proposal mode are likely to consolidate at the outset, while investors tend to do so on a project basis. They appreciate that few of the specific gains of joint investments are embedded at the broad level of "pooling resources."

With their role clarified, investors are ready to proceed. In order to realize a return, they need a tool which will both prompt necessary information for investments and which applicants need for management of projects.

Chapter 7

The Target Plan vs. the Proposal

To replace the proposal, we suggest a document we shall call the target plan. The concept has two origins. One is the for-profit world, where a business plan is developed to both establish the feasibility of a new enterprise and provide an implementation road map. Our second starting point is the framework of strategic planning. While the concept is too often misunderstood and abused, the notion of strategic direction is most useful. In defining the target plan as a derivative of a business plan, we are not attempting to bring the private sector to government. Rather, we believe that tools for seeking outcomes from business can be effectively adapted to investing in the public sector. Indeed, it is one of many ways in which business and government can learn from each other.

While the proposal and the target plan are very different, a comparison is usefully drawn between elements in these documents.

The Proposal	The Target Plan
Needs Statement	The Market/Customers
Goals & Objectives	Performance Targets
Project Description	The Product
Work Plan	Milestones
Staffing Plan	Key Indiviuals
Credentials of Proposing Group	Organization Support
Evaluation Design	Verifications
Line Item Budget	Financial Projections
Letters of Support	Customer Evidence

We now look at the sections which should typically be included in a target plan. Not all elements need be included in all plans and the particular order and wording of sections is not critical. Indeed, some formats can be remarkably short; and even with all elements included, the plan should be shorter than the proposal.

The Market and Your Customers

Define the number and characteristics of the customers your program will serve. Indicate how they are different from the broader population of those with the need you address.

In government, we think in terms of "target population" defined by need. Outcome Funding introduces the concept of the market—those individuals who are potential users of the program offered.

Typical terms to define participants in publicly funded programs include clients, patients, consumers, persons at risk, and violators. We suggest the word *customer*. It may seem an odd label, since persons served by government are often seen as beyond choice, either because they do not have the means to exercise it or because they are bound by mandate or dependency to a given service or enforcement action. But clients are customers precisely because they *do* have a choice. We can offer all the workshops, media campaigns, counseling sessions and other activities that we wish, but if a person does not choose to stop smoking, use a park, avoid pregnancy, find and keep a job, or obey the speed limit, the program cannot achieve its results. In reality, the program is as dependent on participants for its success as the participants are dependent on the program for help. People as customers often have a variety of options available to deal with their needs—including more than one available service.[20]

Since our first edition, we do recognize that the quality movement has "customered" many of us near to death. If you choose a different word, that's fine! In our terms, customers are these people, generally external to an agency, who participate in programs and are expected to gain a benefit and/or undertake to change something.

In proposal logic, needs statements are important to show that the applicant understands the complexity and the depth of the overall problem, as well as its causes. In contrast, the market section focuses not on the need itself but on those who have it. More specifically, it discusses those individuals who the program will serve.

Distinguishing customers from a general population with a given need is a critical part of definition. Projects which state they are equally applicable to all persons within a needs category tend to be less effective than those which are designed specifically for a subset of that population. In government programs, as in suits, one size rarely fits all. If the implementor has not identified and differentiated customers, they literally lack a starting point.

Profile a small cross-section of individuals typical of people to be served by the program. Explain why those people want the program or can be persuaded to try it.

The profile of individuals underscores the essential value of depth over breadth. A critical factor in predicting project success is the extent to which the implementors vividly and deeply know the people they will serve. This is a knowledge shown through specifying who a typical participant is and why they will engage in the program. Reasons why the implementor believes people *need* a project are less relevant than reasons people *want* and will *use* it.

Specify any intermediaries whose involvement is critical for your program to work. Indicate why they will cooperate.

In a surprising number of cases, the first people who must be sold on participation in a program are not its beneficiaries but members of another group without whose involvement the implementor cannot get to the customer. Further, the needs of the intermediary may well be different from that of the "end-user." For example, a program whose product is drug prevention may have an approach that calls for entering public school classrooms to provide important information to children. While it is useful to keep in mind the needs of young people in order to engage them, this cannot be the initial focus. Rather, the very different needs of schools and teachers must first be met if the children are ever to get the message. Teachers need assurance, for example, that this program will, at worst, not add to their workload or make it impossible to cover the required curriculum in the time allowed, and at best, may actually be helpful to student learning.

If a needs statement is to be done, let the investor do it. They know what they require as data so that a balanced set of programs that work effectively at a comprehensive scale. They are the experts on the need. Let the implementors show that they, in turn, are experts on some specific kinds of people who have that need and with whom they will work.

Performance Targets

Specify the performance targets you are committed to achieving, and indicate the reason for not setting lower or higher levels.

In contrast to goals and objectives, which tend to be multiple and broad, results in the target plan are focused and narrow. They speak to what will occur for customers if the program is successful. For health and human service programs, performance targets refer to something that a respondent does as a result of receiving a program service or other form of "treatment." In other cases, the targets refer to the level of customer satisfaction that a particular program achieves, i.e., timelining and completing of applying for a building permit. A program in prenatal services may have as a target that fifty at-risk pregnant women will visit a health clinic regularly before delivery and follow the advice they receive.

Most performance targets can and should be stated in observable terms. "Enhanced self esteem" for pregnant women is not a target until we know what that means. Just what will be different in a person with higher self-esteem?

The second part questions the rationale for the level of target performance. The investor wants to know that the level is set sufficiently high that it will be a real "stretch" for the implementor, and yet not be unrealistic. Success is not necessarily defined as having reached or exceeded a target. In fact, the reverse might be more accurate. In general, this discussion will include a baseline condition, defined as how many of the program customers are likely to achieve a program target without the program.

List any significant secondary effects or consequences which may be associated with reaching your performance target, including adverse as well as beneficial ones.

All projects have the potential to do harm as well as good. A person who stops smoking may also stop drinking—or he/she may gain many unhealthy pounds. In at least some cases, possible side effects can be defined prior to a project when there is time to anticipate strategies to enhance positive consequences and inhibit or avoid negative ones. An in-depth discussion of performance targets and how to define them, is the sole subject of Chapter 12.

The Product

Specify your product, its key features and its comparative advantages over other products offered to achieve the same performance targets and outcomes.

The proposal assumes that the program can be defined as the total of its activities. Reviewers look for aggregates of actions that sum to comprehensiveness. In contrast, the target plan believes in definition by core, not periphery. To get at the essence of what is proposed, investors want something that is clear and as literal as possible. The preferred term is product. Whether in private or public sectors, products mean services as well as goods. Products, unlike processes, cannot be judged successful by their makers. Products have value only in reference to customers who live in a world external to the organization which created them.

Virtually all programs funded by government can be defined in product terms. The Rensselaerville Institute, for example, has long been a national leader in promoting self-help as a way by which communities can get needed housing, as well as such public goods such as water and wastewater systems. The Institute defines self-help as a product, with certain features and a clear sense of the customers to whom it is applicable. It is a product that has an instruction manual, a clear list of benefits to users, and effective packaging. The Institute moved to a product focus after experiencing the limitations of communicating and selling self-help as a program or system. In its early days, The Institute was steeped in the mystique of process. It spoke of the values of self-help and the difficulty of explaining it until one had experienced it. What it learned is that small towns considering the approach wanted to cut through abstractions and learn just what self-help meant to them. They wanted to know exactly how much time they would contribute and what they would gain from it. They also wanted a list of satisfied customers!

Effective products invariably have one or more features that give them a comparative advantage over other products. Many relate to quality. For the product of self-help, for example, The Rensselaerville Institute defines one measure of quality as a minimal cost savings. If a given self-help application cannot save at least 30% over alternate approaches, it has not met its quality standards.

At best, quality definitions become integral in the notion of the product itself. For example, when Caterpillar Tractor states as its mission "48-hour parts service anywhere in the world," it tells you not only its quality standard but also that it is not truly selling equipment at all. It is in the service business, selling reliability of equipment use even in remote locations.

Another kind of feature addresses intensity. In general, some minimal level of a treatment or service is needed before a result can be presumed likely. Without that minimum, the program, from the investor's view, wastes money. This may well suggest that impressively large customer numbers achieved at the expense of reduced intensity may hurt, not help.[21]

Milestones

What are the critical milestones which you must achieve if you are to reach results?

The work plan and deliverables scheduled in the proposal are designed to highlight activity sequence and reports. From the investor perspective, the point of a project is not its documentation anymore than it is the activities documented. The real question for the investor during the project is simpler and more elusive: Is this project on track to achieve its targets? Activity check-off and report completion are poor ways to address this. If compliance were the equivalent of high performance, every teacher who completed next week's lesson plan by Friday at noon would be a brilliant educator.

A much more effective way to track progress toward performance targets is to understand those key accomplishments or threshold points through which project participants must pass if it is to be successful. These are called milestones. The subject is sufficiently important as to warrant detailed discussion as Chapter 13.

Key Individuals

Profile those individuals who will have the most responsibility for shaping your product, connecting it to customers, and achieving performance targets. Focus on energy, capacity, and commitment.

In contrast to the staffing plan approach of the proposal, capacity is not inferred from degrees or seniority. The focus is on the attributes of those who will implement.

In proposals, projects are often "fronted" by well-credentialed people who are designated for leadership roles. Far too often, we weigh the qualifications of high-status leaders when we should be looking at the capacities of the people who will actually deliver the service. In education, for example, proposals are routinely submitted by superintendents, principals, and curriculum specialists when success actually relies on teachers. In banking, senior vice presidents believe that their memos are momentously important when, in reality, customers are far more disposed to do more business at a branch where the tellers remember their name.

Energy as a starting point is vastly underrated in most personnel assessments. Over the course of a project, nothing is more valuable than a key person's ability to infuse life into himself or herself, colleagues, and customers. Energy is less what you need to get started than what you need to keep going. It is also the right stuff for productivity. Energetic people can get twice as much done in a day as non-energetic ones.

Energy has many sources and takes many forms. Often it comes from enthusiasm and high expectations. People who are keenly optimistic about what can happen generally have more energy than those who are pessimistic or even "realistic." This is especially true when the source of optimism is not a generalized faith in the future, but a belief by a person that he or she can make good things happen as a result of personal behavior and factors they can and will control. Energy can also come from a negative. Anger and even outrage for some people sustains an action to redress a wrong.

Capacity comes next. It is a matter of skill and knowledge, not longevity. Whether social worker or business executive, a person with five years' experience is as likely to be high-performing as one with thirty. Indeed, beyond some initial period to "learning the ropes," experience can do as much harm as good. The person whose constant preface is, "I've been doing it this way for twenty years" is not reassuring. In most fields, doing something without change for five years—let alone twenty—is suspect.

Skill and knowledge as keys to capacity should be backed up by specifics. Expressions such as "good with people," or even "well-organized," are meaningless. Skills and knowledge must also be related to project requirements. The search is not for "good people" in a generic sense. It is for the right people for a given project. Specific instructions in the plan can help here. For example, "Name the most important three skills and points of knowledge that you have, and define their contribution to achieving results."

Opportunistic ability is a third factor. While the word is seen by some as a negative, the focus upon seizing opportunities covers a key strength. Timing, for example, can be everything in a project. The right person sees the clock and the calendar as an opportunity for timely interventions; the wrong person sees them as the steady backdrop on which activities are recorded.

A final characteristic is *commitment.* In proposal thinking, commitment quickly becomes viewed as dedication and presumes philosophy and belief. Regretfully, commitment of this nature often reduces to rhetorical fervor. This is not enough.

In the private sector, probably the most important negotiation prior to a final investment decision concerns the ways in which key implementors are locked into the deal. The investor wants to know that the implementor's own assets—home, cars, whatever—are literally on the line. This is done not to create personal hardship but to ensure that the implementor will not sleep easily at night until everything possible has been done that day to achieve results. While this is clearly not appropriate in many programs funded by government, other ways of underscoring tangible commitment are reasonable.

One is a pledge to remain with the program for a given time, barring drastic change in circumstance. At present, many projects experience one or more transitions of key people who take other jobs or leave the area. While the notion of encouraging people to always take opportunities is laudable, this can be highly detrimental to a project. If the investor is committed to financing a program, should not the key people be equally committed to running it?

These attributes are less characteristic of people than points of character. Both investors and implementors should look for the ways in which they run deep in the persons considered for key roles.

If a team approach to managing and/or implementing is used, specify how strengths of individuals are complementary and not duplicative.

Given that most projects require a team, the investor wants to know just how members were selected. In addition to the capabilities of individuals relative to the roles they will play, the focus is on how one person's strengths offset another person's weakness. For example, most projects need a person who is excellent at working with customers to gain the needed result. They also need a person who is excellent at cost control to ensure that the organization does not run out of money between progress payments. Optimally, the human "critical mass" for a project is more likely composed of differences than of similarities. If people share attributes, chances are excellent that one or more is redundant.[22]

Organization Support

Please note the two most similar projects undertaken by the parent agency and the extent to which they stated and achieved performance targets.

In advancing their credentials to sponsor a project, agencies are prone to refer to history and evolution, mission and values, and their full range of programs. From the Outcome perspective, illumination requires a spotlight, not a floodlight. Past performance in similar work is a better predictor of future performance than is any other factor, and must be stated. If past successes featured a cast of characters now departed—and if the person selecting those people has departed as well—this must be noted, since past achievement may then be unconnected to future success.

List the specific resources which the implementing group will contribute to the project and which are critical to success.

This question is a way not only to assess organizational support, but to look at what the agency believes constitutes support. In the conventional proposal approach, a local financial "match" is taken as evidence of implementor commitment. Financial contributions, however, indicate how a project will be financed, not how it will be enabled to achieve outcomes. Unless money is the only needed resource, the budget page is not the place to look for reassurance. One key is contingent commitments. If a project is not achieving its targets, what organizational resources will be deployed to change that?

Note and justify the priority this project has for the implementing agency.

While the organization can assure ten funding sources that its program is "of the highest priority," the plan asks for evidence of time and overhead functions to be dedicated to this project *vis-a-vis* other projects.

As with individuals, the investor also wants to see evidence that the organization cannot lightly walk away from a project that falters. In some instances, this can be accomplished by tying revenue to performance. At the least, some revenue can be deferred until the project has fully achieved its results, in the same way that building owners withhold a retainer until evidence of a trouble-free structure is at hand. A stronger approach is that of performance contracting in which revenues are partially or even entirely dependent on results. This is discussed in Chapter 12.

If financial risk is not appropriate as a way of underscoring priority, we can at least turn to reputational risk. An unambiguous statement of result targets is an important prerequisite for this healthy and motivating vulnerability. Without it, the investor will not know when success is at hand, and will have no way of determining if the project fizzles.

A priority can also include the commitment to ensure that key staff stay the course, even if it means increasing their salary with agency funds to avoid losing them to a better offer.

Verifications

How will you verify the extent to which your performance targets are achieved?

For many programs we recommend that the concept of evaluation be set aside. Formal assessment is costly and often never completed. It also prompts implementors to hide or obfuscate error. Evaluations call for measuring objectives. In Outcome Funding the point is simpler: to verify results.

Verification focuses on customers and, where appropriate, a comparison group. In the most direct approach, customers are asked to determine changes for, to, and by themselves. Methods for validation that encourage higher achievement than would be the case without verification are encouraged. The point is not to measure what happens, but to do everything possible to bias a project toward success.

In most cases, the formulation of performance targets enables direct observation of their presence. A variety of tracking systems can be employed. In those instances where an indicator must be used to signify accomplishments, this will also have been articulated clearly in the statement of a target. Chapter 14 discusses verification in detail.

Financial Projections

Specify project costs on the basis of milestones and performance targets.

The applicant is not (unless absolutely necessary) asked to provide the traditional line item budget at all! Instead they are asked to think in cost-accounting terms. Simply put, costs are distributed or "loaded" onto milestone and target accomplishment. If forty persons are served by a project costing $20,000, the unit *service* cost is $500 per person. If ten of these customers achieve a desired result, the unit *result* cost is $2,000.

One further value of cost-accounting is that it forces out questions about value added from overhead or indirect costs. If the executive director is devoting 15% of his or her time at a cost of $10,000 to a project that enables twenty people to reach a performance target, is the director adding at least $500 of value to each unit of result?

Using a variety of possible formats, implementors can build their budget on the basis of the actual time and expense it will take to get the people they will have in their "hopper" at a given time to a given achievement point. This not only sharpens the thinking of resource allocation but prepares the way for investor payments on the basis of milestone achievement. Without knowing what it is projected to cost, this cannot be done. The real gains, however, are to the implementor, who can now know if they are spending money at a rate that will allow them to get to the finish line. When costs are put on a timeline rather than a progress line, there may be no way of knowing.

In our experience with a variety of groups taking up Outcome Funding, this part of the target plan is the most difficult. The first hurdle is getting implementors to see financial information as a management tool and not solely as a reporting function. The second is to surmount the dreadful legacy of many decades of line item thinking. As with other areas of the approach, the investor is the key. Until they begin to require this kind of information as the basis of progress payments, many groups will continue to say, "It's the second quarter and we've spent within our line items; we're ready for more money."

Complete a cash flow projection using the schedule given for payments on grants.

The final part of the financial projections is critical in the private sector, and almost totally ignored by many government and non-profit groups. This is the cash flow projection. It is an essential tool to enable the investor to know the right schedule for timing investments, and for enabling the implementors to have money when necessary. While many groups funded by government experience long delays in getting funds, most could cope with this situation far better if they had the cash flow tool at their disposal.

It is a prerequisite for cash management—which includes strategies for accelerating receivables and delaying payables. Also, without a cash flow statement, short-term borrowing is difficult. Indeed, there is no way of knowing whether the real problem is cash flow (which is solved when anticipated revenue arrives), or simply cash (which means that expenses are higher than revenue, regardless of timing).

Plan for Self-Reliance

Show how your program will continue without investment from this source.

This section is applicable to those investments in which the intent is to provide seed funding or in other ways to encourage programs to develop ongoing viability. In these instances, the need is for more than a shift from one short-term grant source to another. This may well involve a source of long-term funding that can be secured once the program is proven. User fees and third party payments on a fee-for-service basis are examples. Equally applicable is cost reduction, so that the program can continue at a lower per-customer cost. Indeed, the best way to raise money is to need less of it!

If implementors cannot think of at least some ways to take a viability initiative at the outset, the probability is not high that they will do so later.

Customer Evidence

Provide names of individuals who have expressed a strong interest in being a customer for your program.

A list of five real customers is far more powerful than twenty letters of support, regardless of the power or prestige of the letterheads.

That is the target plan. It is a document that not only responds to investor questions, but becomes an operating plan for implementors. Again, the specific sections included and the wording of sections must be tailored to a given investment area and purpose. So too will the "Request for Plans" vary. We now turn to the matter of how best to review plans once received.

Chapter 8

"Due Diligence"

"Due Diligence" is again a term from business. It is concerned with verifying the accuracy of key representations made by implementors as the basis for investment decisions. If applicants, for example, submit that some customers are ready and eager to use their product, the question is whether the investor can rely on that assertion. If the proposer indicates that he/she is fully capable and strongly "committed" to a project, is there a way to ensure that this is so? "Due Diligence" goes through the plan to the project it represents.

Strategic Guidelines

These seven strategies guide the Due Diligence process:

- **Include independent verification**. In contrast to proposal review, Due Diligence involves research to check out key representations. The premise is less that applicants will deliberately mislead, but that honest personal belief from advocates and supplicants may blend expectation with reality. The target plan suggests that the data needed for such steps can be gotten by a quick call to several persons who are potential customers. There is no substitute for hearing their interest in their own words.

- **Focus on key questions**. While initial sorting may deal with sections of the plan, Due Diligence for the public sector should focus on the questions the investor wants answered. They are:

- How compelling is the performance target and the outcome it will yield?
- How high is the probability that implementors will achieve their target?
- What is the return on investment? How cost effective is this investment compared with others we might make?
- Where does this fit within portfolio needs and other investment objectives?

- **Avoid incremental distinctions**. Fine distinctions are simply not warranted by the applicant's paperwork. What is the difference between getting a "15" or an "18" out of 20 points allocated for a given proposal section? Investors need to focus on distinctions that are simpler and more readily derived. Our concept moves from rating plan elements to sorting them. Plans are literally sorted into piles, using such widely-separated points that reliability (the probability that different respondents would make the same decision) is high. The strategy is to determine extremes and let the middle define itself. Here is a typical Outcome Funding sort, using a three-point spread:

1	2	3
very low	everything in between	very high

- **Seek a singular, not comparative focus**. Unlike the proposal review process, which gets quickly to comparative ratings and rankings, Due Diligence asks that each plan be considered solely on its own merits. Only when that process is completed are comparisons in order. At that point, return on investment comes into play as the measuring stick.

- **Get from paper to players**. To avoid making a variety of inferences about what a grantwriter really meant, hold conversations with key implementors sooner rather than later. Follow-up is not necessary with a grantwriter unless that person will play a direct role in the project and take personal responsibility for achieving results.

- **Bet on the bettors**. In contrast to proposal review, which looks to committees and quantitative schemes to take out personal judgment, Due Diligence honors it. The recording of strong personal feeling by a given investment agent is allowed and a direct connection between the investor and the project is not only allowed but encouraged. Investors often add rigor by asking reviewers to predict the likelihood of success for all projects considered as finalists. Keep score. As with forecasters of sporting events, it is possible to see over time just who is predicting most accurately.

- **Include no more people than are necessary**. The investor believes that incisive judgment is rarely enhanced by great numbers. While there may be other reasons to add reviewers, investors are convinced that one or two people with the capacity to make sound judgments are far more valuable than committee-based decisions. The acid test for adding any individual beyond one to the process is whether he or she truly add value to the quality of the decision.

Steps of Due Diligence

Due Diligence, as we have tested and refined it, generally comprises six steps. This is a general model, not a precise recipe.

1. *Paper Review.* This first step is conducted by one person—joined by another only if that person believes that he/she is unable to unequivocally and promptly complete the sorting. The point is to assess the extent to which the plan is responsive to the information requested and to identify areas where it is not. In this stage, responders look solely for completeness of response, not for whether they agree with the answers or not. Also, no value is given for length. The focus is on *customer profile, performance targets,* and *product definition.* The only reason for setting plans aside at this point is that they are not responsive to investor intent (interest to the investor), or are incomplete. Even here, the reviewer may choose to keep the submission in the hopper if it is felt that there is the hint of either a good product or a very good implementor.

2. *The Telephone Interview.* A telephone conversation immediately follows Step #1, and is generally conducted by the same person who provided the paper review. It gives the plan's implementing agent a chance to add information and clarify any confusions. Information received by phone is given no less weight than information received in writing. The investor wants to confirm not only that the proposal is clear, but that it is at least minimally acceptable in terms of its performance target.

   When the phone call ends, the investor can set aside the lowest-sorted plans, using a score point from the sorts made. We recommend that about twice the many plans be kept in the hopper as can be financed.

   At the end of the telephone conversation, applicants should have two reactions. First, the organization has been responsive to them in the sense that someone has read their plan carefully and contacted them promptly. Second, they have had every opportunity to clarify and to amplify what was said in writing, and have assurance that they will not be bumped out either on a technicality or because they simply do not write well. The investor approach ensures a remarkably high degree of satisfaction even by those who are not selected for funding.

3. *Personal Interviews.* At this point, an interview is scheduled to include the project director and a senior responsible agent from the implementing organization. This is distinct from a site visit and is often best removed from the applicant's setting. The point is to concentrate on the proposing organization and its project, not to "feel" the realities of a given site. Site visits confuse need with response and introduce the roles of host and guest, which make it difficult to ask and answer tough questions. Also, as clever grant recipients have known for years, they can be fully orchestrated.

This step is costly, in that a team can interview no more than five to six groups in a day. It often involves fewer hours, however, than the extensive scrutiny by multiple eyes of the written paper. More importantly, it is indispensable for making the right selections.

We recommend a team of two to three persons, including the initial reviewer and those with both program and fiscal knowledge. Each interviewer becomes a specialist in one primary area of inquiry and is given latitude to probe deeply. Those interviewed are not asked to elaborate on their applications, but rather are asked immediately about those areas needing clarification.

Some questions will be standard for all interviews and others will be suggested by each plan. Among the former are some proven ways of testing representations in key areas. For example, to gauge the project director's personal commitment to results, this question is useful: "May we remember your name?" When the respondent asks what is meant by the question, continue in this vein: "When results are recorded, they are usually connected to an organization. In this case, our memory trace will be of you. We will remember your name in connection with the performance targets you achieved or did not achieve. Is that all right with you?"

Following the interview, individual interviewer impressions and then group conclusions are recorded. At this point, a very high, very low, or "in between" designation is given in three areas:

- **Performance targets**—How clear and compelling are they?
- **Probability**—What is likelihood that the performance targets will be achieved, at least in significant measure, by the implementor?
- **Return on Investment**—To what extent does the project reflect an impressive relationship between dollars in and results out?

A second set-aside is now done for those proposals sorted as low on any dimension.

4. *Verifications.* This step involves speaking to individuals best in a position to substantiate and clarify key representations made in plans still in the hopper, when an outside perspective is needed. This

is not a "reference check," which seeks to verify character. Any substantial discrepancy between key representations made by the proposer and evidence from another source is recorded, and if the discrepancy is in an area deemed critical to the project's success, the plan is taken out of consideration. An interim step of further discussion with the proposer to understand the discrepancy, may first be taken if there is sufficient time and desire.

Discrepancies are serious for two reasons. First, if a proposal is relying on a key assumption which is not accurate, the likelihood that the project will succeed is dramatically reduced. Second, if an applicant is unable to accurately understand one key element of his or her project or its environment, further misconceptions may well arise as the project unfolds.

5. *Selections.* With interviews and verification complete, selections are made. This is the first point at which projects are compared. Our suggested starting point is the use of grids which array projects along the critical dimensions of result, probability, and cost-effectiveness. For example:

PERFORMANCE TARGETS

Probability of Reaching Targets:	**Very High**	**In Between**	**Very Low**
Very High			
In Between			
Very Low			

In those instances where more projects score highest (e.g., in the top left cell of this grid) than can be supported, several strategies can be used. One is to consider the strength rather than the breadth of feeling. If a given investor in the interview process feels strongly that a sort category should be higher than that determined by the group, he/she adds a "plus" to the three numbers used to reflect the category. That becomes an additional sort as needed. A second strategy is "value adding." In some instances, a project may offer a special advantage not captured in the criteria of focus. In general, these will be factors we could call "portfolio enhancement," in that they will meet a secondary investment objective.

Note that the selection process retains a quantitative framework, and remains fully defensible. It is simply that the numbers are built on sorts rather than ratings.

6. *Contracting*. In Due Diligence, this step is considered part of the selection process rather than a perfunctory, if prolonged, activity performed after groups have been chosen. In contracting, the focus shifts to the finalization of milestones and progress payments based upon their completion. Additional specificity on verification of results may also take place. Contracting is a final developmental step to ensure that investor and implementor understand their commitments in legally-binding form. Even at this point, it should be perfectly acceptable for either party to conclude that the investment should not take place.

7. *Turndowns*. This step is generally considered so unimportant, or at least routine, that a form letter will do nicely. Yet this is just the point at which the

investor can not only improve future applications, but convert negative to positive feelings. All that is needed is a communication that is personalized in two ways. The first way is to praise something in the application that warrants it. The second way is to give critical feedback so that the applicant can improve his/her proposal next time.

Such personal responses are generally not given, on the theory that they will open the doors to dissatisfied calls from groups and perhaps their legislators. But this has not been our experience. Indeed, dissatisfaction is strongest when there is absolutely no feedback which the person can use to rationalize defeat or to gain investment in the future. Giving out bad news at the earliest possible moment also helps to manage dissent.

If a typical proposal requires some 15-30 person hours to review, how long should a target plan take in Due Diligence? The following general time frames are realistic.

Step	Person Hours
Initial Processing	.5 – 1
Paper review	.5 – 1
Telephone interview and finalist determination	1 - 2
Personal Interview	3 - 6
Verifications	1 - 2
Selection	2 - 4
Total:	8 - 16

The first point of this reduced time is that the initial paper is shorter. This not only reduces the expense of photocopying and distribution, but greatly shortens the time needed for initial reading. The second point is the way in which the structure ensures that the most time-consuming steps are not applied to all target plans. Time is concentrated only on those plans that justify it.

A problem often raised concerns the reviewer insistence on talking to a lead project implementor. Groups in many instances cannot afford to hire this person until the investment commitment is made. In descending order of desirability, here are some options for dealing with this matter:

- *Encourage a contingent employment commitment.* Ask the implementor to define key people who will agree to work on the project if financed. Agree not to jeopardize their present positions in the course of Due Diligence.

- *Make a contingent investment decision.* The contingency is acceptability of the key people to be selected. So long as there are clear and shared expectations of the necessary qualities needed, this should not be an undue hardship or uncertainty.

- *Focus on the selector.* While not as effective, a fall-back position might assess the individual who will choose key staff. In addition to understanding the criteria, comfort is gained when the selector knows that the investor will hold him or her accountable for both selections and for taking steps to replace people if necessary.

In the investment approach, the announcement of the award is only the beginning. And indeed, what happens next can be more consequential than accuracy in making that determination. This is the matter to which we now turn.

Chapter 9

Supporting the Investment

In the conventional approach to funding by government, the word used for the post-grant period is "monitoring," and the outcome most sought is accountability. The monitor ensures not only compliance, but documentation of compliance. When the funder moves to a program interest, it is generally in a developmental role designed to nurture and build organizations that it has funded. The activities are called "technical assistance" and "capacity building," and are often introduced when a widespread or generic problem is perceived.

Outcome Funding has a different focus because it has a different point. It is not only less concerned with inputs than with outcomes, but less concerned with helping organizations than in supporting projects. While these objectives assuredly intertwine, the investor would rarely justify efforts to help a group that did not have clear and direct payoffs from the project it has financed.

The Investor Role

When an investment decision is made, interdependence is created. The investor and recipient are mutually reliant on each other to achieve results. They are in the same boat, and it is futile to believe that the other end might sink. Traditionally, both funder and implementor view the funder's only asset as money, and its only sanction as the ability to stop providing it. This behavior is guided by a mistaken presumption that the full amount of the grant is an entitlement. While the investor approach conveys the expectation of full investment, it does not promise it. Future payments must be earned on the basis of progress toward performance targets. At the same time, implementors need not worry that the investor will capriciously withhold more funds, since this would assuredly limit, if not eliminate, satisfactory return on the dollars already expended.

Investor support of projects financed can be understood in terms of three dimensions, each discussed below.

Anticipate problems. Most implementors are the last to see major problems on the horizon. They are simply too caught up in the day-to-day events, and perhaps blinded by conviction and/or commitment. Because of this, the investor's involved but distanced perspective becomes a key "early warning" resource to the implementor. When problems are discovered after they happen, the cost of dealing with them soars. Ironically, a social and human support system that puts so much stress on prevention for at-risk *clients* fails to honor the value of prevention for at-risk *projects*.

Provide help. The investor's first and continuing question should be, "How can I help?" Investors have a surprising number of resources, including these:

- *Influence*. If a school chooses not to cooperate with a drug-prevention program, a call from the investor who also provides funds to those schools may elicit a different response. This can often work when a problem arises with roadblocks inadvertently created by other agencies in government. As a last recourse, government investors in some cases can directly influence clients to whom they offer other benefits.

- *Knowledge*. Investors can connect implementors to experiences elsewhere, which can avoid many painful reinventings. They also have knowledge of theories and research which may enlighten program performance or forecast results from different strategies. Indeed, if the implementor is operating without benefit of any significant information or relevant insight known to the investor, this critical role is not being fully used.

- *Flexibility*. Often the help implementors need most is in dealing with the investor's own rules. Flexibility on procedural changes, such as shifting funds between budget lines without extensive justification, may prove critical, as might a waiver of procedural guidelines which do not promote results. Flexibility also ensures that implementors are not locked into work plans. The most critical permission can be the permission to change course.

Avoid Micro-Monitoring. Some grant makers, even with very small sums involved, have a hard time in not following their money out the door. This is a mistake. The investor is *not* the implementor and should thoroughly resist efforts to control at a procedural or activity level. Once a performance target is clear, leave the implementors to achieve it. Control of the results is much more critical than control of inputs. This guideline is especially critical when grants officers are responsible for a large number of investments. If done well, Outcome Funding will not increase the investor time loading on projects once financed—and may well reduce it.

Intervene when necessary. When anticipation of

problems and help falls short, the investor has two options. One is to disinvest and cut losses. The other is to intervene either directly or through a third party. Banks and venture capitalists employ "turn-around" specialists who have the authority to intervene in the project. A typical presumption is that if the project remains off-track, the reason probably lies with the key people. Intervention generally leads to staff replacement or substantial augmentation.

Intervention in this context is very different from the intervention now undertaken by public agency contract and program officers. When funders second-guess travel or supply requests, or become heavy-handed about the way they believe things should be done, they mistakenly shift the burden of management to themselves. This is the same problem as seen with school boards and organization directors who fail to honor the line between policy and program. Investors have no desire to tell others how to run their project. They simply want to ensure that the right people are in place to do so.

Toward Investor Agents

As with project selection, time—for the investor after decisions are made—goes in different and more selective directions. In Outcome Funding, procedural requirements which are not absolutely necessary as legal protection and not directly related to the achievement of results are dropped. Who cares whether the implementor bought the pencils or a consultant's time...as long as it reached its target?

As with project scrutiny, the key to effective investor support is neither a body of knowledge nor a person. The qualities of a good investor agent are, in general, similar to those sought in the project director. Energy, capacity, and commitment are critical. At the same time, an added virtue is restraint. Investor agents achieve results not by their own actions, but through those of others. This, incidentally, is the generic definition of a manager.

In the previous chapter, we underscored the importance of betting on the bettor. Here the same logic holds, because investors rely on the capabilities of their investor agents, i.e., contract managers or grant officers. Wherever possible, the selector should become the agent. The message is then unmistakable: "You suggested that we finance this one. Now, make sure it works."

Agent support can make the difference between project success and failure, and high-capability people must be chosen for this role. Indeed, an average project selection coupled with an excellent investor agent can be a more potent combination than an outstanding choice and a weak agent.

One might well apply the investor approach itself to the task of selecting the right investment agents. How well do they know their customers (implementors for whom they have responsibility)? What products (as opposed to processes or procedures) do they offer these customers? What are their own performance targets in terms of enabling implementor success?

Many organizations are concerned with whether grant tracking should occur from a program or a contracts office. If the focus is on performance targets and outcomes, it does not matter. What is consequential is not place in the structure but match-up of skills. Where possible, the investor agent should be chosen to offset any weakness uncovered in the course of making the decision to finance. On the one hand, if a group is seen as strong on direct program skills but weak on organization and financing, an agent with skills in the latter is essential. On the other hand, a well-organized and fiscally-prudent implementor lacking "spark" may need a cheerleader with high energy and expectations.

The investor agent's role is a shifting one. On the one hand, agents will find that some programs are on course and need little time, while others are clearly in trouble and need help. Conversely, they will find that the kind of help which is needed varies greatly, not only in content but in approach. An implementor resisting evidence that his or her program has a problem may need an abrupt and forceful message, while one losing confidence against tough odds may need the investor's encouragement.

As discussed in Chapter 13, the milestone is the key support tool in the Outcome focus. It specifies those things that must be accomplished if a performance target is to be met. If accurate, milestones are not only important but integral. They must be met if the result is to occur. Brief quarterly reports should stress literal and specific performance in achieving milestones. A report format might look as follows:

> In no more than one page each, state whether you have reached specified milestones. For any milestone which is not reached, please tell us: 1) why you did not reach it, and 2) what you have done to make course corrections. In those instances in which you no longer believe the milestone to be appropriate in either nature or degree, tell us why and specify a better milestone to forecast successful achievement of performance targets. We do not want long explanations.

Honesty is an important expectation and requirement. Implementors need to know that the only unacceptable behavior is failure to report on a problem that is interfering with results. A negative surprise should never happen at the end of the project period. At the same time, a shortfall on milestones is not necessarily the end of the world. When a milestone is not reached, there can be several reasons: a) the group is underperforming for some specific reason; b) the milestone is unrealistic—and perhaps indicative of an unrealistic performance target as well; or c) the milestone is the wrong one on which to have focused. Until the reason is determined, the investment agent has no way of knowing what kind of help is needed.

In Due Diligence review, we stressed the need to follow-up a brief examination on paper with a prompt telephone call in order to avoid making unwarranted inferences. The same strategy holds true in investment support. Periodic calls need only take 10-15 minutes each to remind the implementor of the partner's readiness to help, and to get an update on milestone achievement. If follow-up is needed, it should happen immediately. Alacrity is also needed when the written reports come in. In conventional funding, the implementor learns in due course if the forms submitted are complete. In Outcome Funding, the implementor should learn promptly if his or her performance is in doubt or jeopardy.[23]

If a problem emerges, a longer telephone call may well be indicated, often followed by a site visit. Traditionally, when problems emerge, great energy and time goes into rationalizing the failure—generally by pointing to external factors as the problem. In Outcome Funding, bad luck and low-performance explanations are virtually irrelevant except as recognition of determination to overcome the barrier. Attention should focus on what is being done by implementors to change *their* behavior to achieve the highest possible results.

When the project is concluded, the investment agent asks for verification of results. The focus is on what happened to those individuals directly served by the program. Where possible, tangible evidence of behavioral change or other performance should be presented.

A final step in project close-out is a written or oral report, in which implementors contribute learnings to their colleagues and the investor. Learning is a primary investor agenda, and its meanings and strategies are discussed in Chapter 15.

Chapter 10:

Outcome Budgeting

Outcomes are as critical in public sector operations as in the activities they fund. Cities such as Sunnyvale, California have clearly shown that it is possible to move from the number of people employed in public works to the cost per pothole repaired. Governments are now learning how to measure outputs in social and human services, having persuaded not only themselves but the voters that it is not the number of books or acres of park in inventory that matter but rather frequency of use and customer satisfaction.[24]

As a form of Outcome Funding, budgeting can use many of the same concepts described in Chapters 6 - 9 on grantmaking. At the same time, the focus is distinct. The plan developed to gain financing for a project is somewhat different from the plan designed to gain financing for an organization or organizational unit. One element of difference is that bureaus and departments of government tend to be deluged with planning requirements--from strategic to quality. A target plan to replace a budget request must find a way to displace some other forms of planning, each of which has its advocates and vested supporters.

We also caution that grafting a new proposal or review format to an existing budget system will simply add paper to an already overstuffed pursuit. Most major efforts to reform budgeting end in a default position that looks in practice much like the system they were designed to replace. The reason: they fail to grasp the profound need for the mindset shift from funder to investor. As Osborne and Gaebler point out, we have long been preoccupied with the question of how much government we should have, when the real question is what kind of government we should have.

Our contention is that an investing-based government is very different than a funding-based government. At the moment, when more money is found, the response from an agency is, "Great, we can keep those 20 people slated for layoffs." How much better to hear, "Super, we can increase our results."

Budgeting as Investment

The investing notion must first deal with the concept of control, a function that drives much of the procedural review and monitoring of budgets and their expenditure at present. Outcome Funding does not ask governments to "lose control" of their money but, rather to shift control from a focus on inputs to a focus on outcomes. The point is to look at what money buys.

Why should it matter to senior leaders how money is shifted among line items or realigned as long as the expenses are legal and as long as the target is hit? With control at the results level, leaders need not pace their operating units. Rather, they can look at critical points to ensure units are on course to achieve their target, then wait for them at the finish line. Our control contention is that it is better to know where someone is going than to know what they are doing.[25]

Outcome budgeting is also inherently more entrepreneurial in its flexibility on inputs. People are not locked into mindless steps along an original workplan. Beyond this, effective investment principles suggest that if an agency or bureau can hit its target with less money than anticipated, the investment should be left in place such as to build more capacity and reward high performance. At present, the consequence for excellence is too often the call-back of unexpended funds. Funders seek barriers; investors seek incentives.

Governments now entering the realm of performance-based budgeting tend to stop short of the full outcome line. One common practice is to focus on what are termed "outputs"--generally defined as units of service or delivery. This moves in the right direction by going beyond measuring dollars, staff, and other resources going in. But in our terms, the target is not the activity but, rather, what happens to, with, or for people as a result of using the activity. In some cases, even customer satisfaction is not enough. We all know people who leave conferences feeling highly satisfied (especially if they gave a talk) but with no evidence that the meeting accomplished anything.

What are the benefits to the public sector of shifting to the investment approach for internal as well as external operations? A foremost virtue is an ability to sell the public on the basis of results. Increasingly, evidence abounds that when government can lead from accomplishment rather than activity it gains much stronger taxpayer support, from conservatives and liberals alike.

A second gain lies in focusing. The public sector finds it difficult to say no to new programs--especially if prompted by urgent need or a strong constituency. Most governments are involved in a far greater range of activities than even our most diverse corporations would entertain. They either find it hard to stick to their knitting or are uncertain what their core business truly is. The ability to gauge return can not only make it easier to stop taking on new programs that do not make results sense but to stop investment in existing programs that have a low return. In part, the power of this tool lies in the ability to compare investment opportunities, as most of us do in our private lives.

Outcome Funding for budgets as well as for grants, however, is neither a science nor a panacea. It boils down to judgement far more than to numerical score.

The notion of return on investment is complex in budgeting, given that the objectives of the operating unit and of government as a whole are distinct. A given agency looks at its own performance, while a state, county or city government is looking at the net effect of all programs. A higher cost in job creation, for example, may lead to lower costs for the welfare and health departments. An even greater red herring enters when programs are federally supported. Activities for persons with disabilities that can be made Medicare-eligible strongly reduce state tax support, while increasing the cost at the national level.

As another complexity, life cycle costs—whether for a road or a building—are often very different from capital costs alone. Endurance also pertains to the length of a problem. With life cycle costing, the expense to prevent a drug user, a fire, or an illiterate person gains relative value over the cost to deal long term with one of these conditions, once in place.

Perhaps the biggest implication of Outcome Budgeting is that it connects money and results. The consequence of this connection is that budgeting becomes a programmatic as well as a financial matter. Indeed, it becomes the most critical form of planning. It is nonsensical and incredibly wasteful and burdensome to have separate budgets, strategic plans, mission statements, and quality plans. The target plan or business plan can incorporate them all. And should!

Boundary Conditions for Budgets

We asked the staff of a large North Carolina county with

which we have worked to specify the criteria that an ideal budgeting system should meet. Their responses form eight key points:

1. It should be simple, clear, understandable. This translates to:
   - letting us take less time to do it;
   - letting us answer questions people ask us.

2. It should not be paper-intensive. It should include only the information that is really needed. This translate to:
   - less time in preparation;
   - letting us use it as a management tool.

3. It should be flexible. This translates to:
   - meeting new needs that arise;
   - making changes as gain experience over a year.

4. It is realistic. This translates to:
   - having enough money to get the job done;
   - separating mandates and options; wants and needs.

5. It is meaningful to all levels of the organization. This translates to:
   - ensuring that no one is asked to work with a budget they had no hand in preparing;
   - building a widely shared responsibility for money.

6. It is a natural part of the planning process, not an added element. This translates to:
   - streamlining instead of bureaucratizing;
   - making budgeting part of our work life.

7. It is useful for achievement. This translates to:
   - effective work planning and implementation;
   - expense control;
   - performance assessment.

8. It reflects customer and stakeholder priorities in a fair way. This translates to:
   - equity, as broadly defined;
   - a clear sense that money is best achieving the public interest as distinct from the addition of private interests.

These are most useful boundary conditions. Number seven goes to the heart of Outcome budgeting, which is not to improve accountability but to improve results. This can only be done when people use budgets as a management tool rather than as an estimating and reporting framework.

The Outcome Budget Template

Many of the elements described in Chapter 7 for the project target plan are relevant to target plans for on-going operations as well. It is equally important to define market and customers, whether optional or mandatory. It is just as critical to define targets and ways of verifying them.

Two new elements of a target plan seeking internal investment for an organizational operation may be useful: The first is a section characterizing the nature of the entity. Its focus: what business are you in?

Three modes are available to define any enterprise. The first is definition by who we *are*. (We are an elementary school with 240 students.) The second is definition by what we *do*. (We provide a full set of educational services to meet all state and local curriculum requirements.) The third and most powerful is definition by achievement. (We enable our students to learn all needed content and tools for effective problem-solving and joyful living.) In this section, respondents are asked to define themselves in accomplishment and directional terms.

When Caterpillar tractor was known by "48 hour parts service anywhere in the world" they clearly positioned themselves as being in the service business--providing equipment that was always useable. When a laundromat owner defined himself as being in the coin business rather than in the cleaning business, he rightly expanded to vending machines rather than dry-cleaning. His core technology was about distributing,collecting, and accounting for quarters. The same kind of focus is most helpful for human services. What is the business of a county food-stamps operation? And how could it best define itself by accomplishment? It also applies to internal units. What is the success of the personnel department?

This question does not require pages. The New York State Division of Parole has a simple statement to define by accomplishment: "Changing the Odds." Rather then being in the business of monitoring parolees and sending them back to jail if they screw up, or of supporting paroles with programs to help them thrive, this agency assumes that the odds are now stacked against the parole making it. Their point is to changes those odds.

Definition by accomplishment can also be profile by vision. Many groups labor mightily on mission statements and conclude (often after prolonged deliberation) that their mission is to provide quality day care or the best possible education. Ho-hum. Visions for investors as well as implementors are much more potent. They work as a pin prick, accentuating the gap between what is and what should be. For investors, it is much better to have a restive and constantly improving organization than a readily contented one. Direction can be even more critical than purpose.

We again stress these components are recommended for a target plan which replaces the diverse and often disconnected current planning and reporting frameworks overlaid on line operations.

A second new section is needed in many Outcome Budgeting contexts to mark the difference between on-going operations and efforts to change them. The fashionable label for this general theme is quality. We prefer the heading of innovation with two elements within it:

Continuous Improvement. Enter total quality and management. How does the operation continually and explicitly work to make its existing operations more efficient and effective? Quality is often seen as a broader umbrella but its limitations are now becoming clear—many from practice but a few from theory. [26]

New Product Development. In the private sector, a significant percentage of revenues is set aside for research and development to create new products. Indeed, one definition of a healthy private sector company is that a high proportion of its revenues come from products introduced within the last five years. Contrast this with the public sector, in which our products in areas ranging from education to public housing to drug prevention have changed remarkably little over decades. [27] In this section, the operation indicates what it is doing to design new products or to import and test them.

While the continuous improvement or evolutionary part of innovation can be funded out of the operating budget, we recommend that the component of new product development be presented at a separate investment window. One reason is that the targets for innovation are different than those from on-going operations, as we discuss more fully in Chapter 17.

The financial section of the target plan for grant seekers remains at the core when this tool is used for budgeting. One useful format is the income statement. The income statement focuses energy not only on the "bottom line" of net performance but on the strategies for improving the financial outcome. Alternative sources of revenue and of cost reduction have equal input and such distinctions as fixed and variable costs can more readily be seen. [28]

One other element in the financial section of the plan will prove of strong value. The first addresses marginal costs. If an investor chose to give an operating unit more money, it could presumably add results at a lower per achievement rate than for its core budget--at least until a certain volume or scale is reached that might trigger more overhead. Cost per achievement will also vary with less money. Notations on the added or "marginal" costs are critical for investor consideration. This area is sufficiently complex to warrant a more thorough discussion. We are thus now writing a companion volume to *Outcome Funding* called *Outcome Finance.*

Budget Review

The same integration of money and program achievement is needed in reviewing budget plans as in drafting them. Further, it is not useful to have separate financial and program reviews with scores then added. This totally misses the point. Costs only have meaning in terms of what return the investment will bring.

At the moment, budgets are reviewed from four reference points: *past expenditures* (subtract 2%; add 4%); *units of service* (a park now open six days a week can be expanded to seven or reduced to five); *timing* (an expenditure can be deferred or accelerated to shape costs); and *political considerations* (including the needs of geographically-elected leaders, the degree of visible squeak in the wheels, and potential for public outcry). Outcome Funding does not fully displace these criteria. It simply adds the dimension of results and returns.

Review of budgets needs the same kind of "due diligence" as do grants. In many situations, we urge that the reviewer be a person new to the operation to avoid the dynamics and complacency of longer term budget review relationships. The same kind of simple three-category sorts are useful as discussed in Chapter 8. They improve reliability and provide the reassurance of numerical systems. At the same time, they encourage funding less by the numbers than by good judgement.

As budgets are finalized, a key investor step is to interact with the operating unit to ensure that they have every opportunity to comment on proposed changes and to own their budget plan. Without ownership, plans will assuredly not be used as management tools.

A second requirement is that the criteria for budget decisions be made explicit. In part this means separating the relative dimensions of need, timing, past spending, political influences, and assessment of performance targets. It also implies that whatever framework the investor is using to define returns be clear and equitably applied.

Supporting the Budget

Budget plans must be tracked, in a way that compares actual performance with budgeted performance as well as with anticipated milestone accomplishments. Without this step, budgets are of little value for any other purpose than to set spending levels. A variety of computer formats which are available for doing this avoids much of the monotony of calculations.

We recommend that the tracking of the budget plan be done at a reasonably small and decentralized scale. This is the level at which course corrections to adjust expenses relative to achievement are most possible. At the Conference Center of The Rensselaerville Institute, for example, a recent analysis of a monthly performance showed that the reason linen costs were higher than budgeted was that more groups had been channeled into buildings with double beds--which cost $0.68 more to clean than single beds. A manager can use that information to make course corrections. In finance, small change adds up to big savings.

We also encourage the use of limited points rather than voluminous data. The acid test for including any data in an information base (whether about money or anything else) is whether anyone is going to use that data to do anything differently. The worst reason for adding data to budgets is the sentiment that someone might at some point want to know it.

One reason that budgets and gains for customers fit so well together is that both have in common the character of operating best at very large and very small levels. At the macro scale, a public agency is preoccupied with balancing total revenues and expenses. But at the micro level, where people live and work in organizations, the opportunity for course corrections is actually much higher than at the top. The further one gets toward service delivery and customers, the more money and achievement are inseparable.

Chapter 11

Getting Started

Let's assume that Outcome Funding makes sense to you and that you want to try it. Your strategy depends on whether you are investor or implementor. Let's start with the investor— whether in grants or budgets.

Whether you are a commissioner, a bureau head, or play any role in the grantmaking process in a public agency, recognize that you are sitting in the right place. Those individuals responsible for drafting the RFP truly have the power to change this system. Few documents from government are more carefully read! And one result is already clear: you will get what you promote. Our advice follows:

Pick a Starting Point. Change requires a place to begin. One place is current problems with RFP cycles. Here are some possibilities:

- *"We can't get contracts out on time."* When contracts begin to back up given the incredible emphasis placed on paperwork, the logic of a new approach can make sense.

- *"Too much power is shifting to contracts or to program people."* The point of Outcome Funding is not to make either program or financial decisions. It is to get these perspectives together to make investment decisions.

- *"We see the same old proposals and grantees each year."* This sentiment suggests a new approach:

to break out of routines which favor those already involved. Outcome Funding is a proven way to encourage new vendors and providers.[29]

- *"The problems we are funding don't seem to get any better."* This acknowledgement suggests that a fine tuning of present program models is not enough. Outcome Funding can be introduced as a tool for innovation and change.

Another strategy is to focus on the virtue of the new approach that will tie to a particular interest. This might be:

- Getting more results for dollars invested—a far more effective way to get "more for less" than haranguing staff to do more each day;

- Deepening the capacity of organizations which compete for funding;

- Broadening the range of solutions applied to tough problems;

- Reducing the time needed per investment decision.

Alternatively, consider human resource development as the entry point. Personal judgment in the investment process energizes people by honoring their capacity to make important decisions and encourages them to remain energized by playing a more direct role in supporting investment to ensure that the result is secured. Use whatever rationale that will gain sufficient support to start. Once in place, the values of Outcome Funding will become self-evident.

Finally, consider the private-sector analogy. If your senior managers pride themselves on being business-like, you might point out that the conventional funding process ignores some powerful tools from the private sector. The target plan, entrepreneurs, and cost accounting also play key roles in the Outcome approach.

Try It At a Small Scale. Many people are strongly vested in the conventional grantmaking process. It provides employment, control, and routine. The best way to loosen the restraints is not to suggest a wholesale change. Rather, speak of the need to develop a prototype which will test, on a small scale, the abilities of the new approach to outperform the RFP system. One prototype might be to take a small pot of money and use the new approach. Another, which we often favor, is to take a portion of the small grant program and use the new approach side-by-side with the old one. This can allow for a very direct comparison of costs and benefits—both short-term and longer-range.[30]

Anticipate Roadblocks. Here is a short list of obstacles which will be raised and how to deal with them.

- *Contracts management people will object to a perceived loss of control.* The presumption is that those who control information are in the driver's seat. Your response: Don't ask people to give up power. Rather, help them to see that accountability and their control functions actually increase. People gain the power to achieve outcomes. Another strategy is to form investment teams which are comprised of program, contracts, and budget people. This can prove the wisdom of a new order before you shake up the old one.

- *Program people will object that performance targets are not appropriate for their human services.* Your response is that each and every program—including such "soft" areas as prevention—can get to a clear statement of results. Recognize that when program people offer this resistance, it is often because they are concerned for their own welfare, not that of the providers they fund. You need to dwell on the benefits to program departments, including competitive advantage in ever more scarce government appropriations.

- *Grantees will strongly resist.* The presumption is that non-profit groups and other vendors socialized to proposals will strongly resist change, especially if they lose a competitive advantage held in conventional grantsmanship. Our experience is that many program deliverers strongly support the change! They now spend hundreds of hours on proposal preparation, site visits, and procedural compliance. The Outcome approach is far less burdensome.

- *No data will exist to defend funding decisions to auditors or to groups not funded.* The sorting tool defined in Chapter 7 continues to provide numbers and a "score." Indeed, reliability (respondent-to-respondent similarity) is actually much higher in the sorting process than in more elaborate weighing systems. Also, documentation on investor judgment is perfectly possible to maintain. The image that the outcome approach is a "loose" system is not accurate.

- *Punitive responses are possible.* The concern is that the investor can withhold funds or in other ways penalize groups which fall short of their targets. One response is a hold-harmless provision for a transition year. The more important assumption, however, is that something which has been granted can then be withdrawn. In the Outcome approach, the only entitlement is the first payment. Everything else is earned under clear and fair guidelines.

- *Outcome Funding leads to creaming; those with the highest needs will not be served.* Selectivity in who is served is entirely within the control of the investor, who can establish priorities by tying level of investment to the degree of difficulty in establishing change.

Treat Outcome Budgeting Separately.
While the tools are similar, the context of internal budgeting is very different from that of external grant making. Among the differences:

- The investment is not in projects but in on-going operations. It is harder to provide starting and ending points than with a discrete project. Also organizations are enmeshed in total quality management, strategic planning, and many other pursuits. While none of these activities are explicitly designed to justify investment, they take up great time, leading many operating units to resent any additional "paperwork" intrusions.

- Many public sector activities cannot be discontinued regardless of performance. County and local governments, for example, are mandated to provide certain essential services. From food stamps and medicare to permits and traffic tickets, government cannot choose to disinvest. Under such conditions, the use of target plans has less apparent incentive.

- Budgets are tied to organizational structure. Unlike grants, budget appropriations are anchored in the strongest traditions and conventions of public agencies. These include not only public expectations and the typical forms of political influence but many forms of management control. Organizations are often budget driven and if the budget is eliminated, the course is not always clear.

- Bad news may be unacceptable. If grant recipients fall short of performance targets, the impacts on the investor are minimal. If internal units fail to perform with taxpayer dollars, however, the political consequences can be profound. Indeed, many people in corrections believe that if the public truly knew the dismal picture on rates of recidivism—particularly for juvenile offenders—that they would be very upset. Outcome or performance-based budgeting will make such shortfalls more apparent.

  These differences should be acknowledged as the basis for effective action. One tactic, for example, for dealing with the problem of overlapping planning frameworks is to sell the target plan on the basis not of value to the organization but of benefit to the using group. In no application is the shift of purpose from better reporting to better management more critical.

If you are a grant recipient rather than an investor, how can you best use this book? We have two answers. First, give a copy to your funders and ask them to discuss it with you. Given their likely inference that you will resist such an approach, you can spark change by indicating that you welcome it. And by initiating the process, you can remain involved. Second, you can use many outcome tools even if your funder does not. We recommend these initial points of emphasis as having the most immediate effect on morale as well as productivity of your group in outcome terms.

- Defining your participants as customers and your program in product terms. This can add clarity where it really counts. Indeed, it is an excellent way to make such terms as "mission" and "quality" come alive for your people and those you serve.

- Specifying performance targets. Even if your funder does not want achievement in Outcome terms, you do. For one or several projects, get in the habit of setting targets to which project staff are strongly committed. Then let activities rather than goals do the adjusting.

Whether as grant recipient or funder, a considerable body of experience is available to help you. The Innovation Group of The Rensselaerville Institute, for example, has developed a number of forms and formats for such steps as defining investor outcomes, drafting Requests for Proposals, reviewing plans, and defining and using milestones.[31]

Outcome Funding, of course, is more than a matter of completing new forms. It is a new way of thinking and acting. It begins and ends at a different place while staying in familiar territory. As Proust observed, the real voyage of discovery consists not in seeking new landscape, but in having new eyes.

15.Thomas Miller, who heads that part of the Ford Foundation which makes Program Related Investments, was executive director of Kentucky Highlands Investment Corporation. His case study of this group is to be called, "Of These Hills."

16. Other elevated notions to avoid include "planting seeds" (to gain unspecified future yields) and the proposition that no cost is too great if just one life has been saved or helped. Neither is helpful at furthering investor logic—nor performance.

17. In the hundreds of public projects we have reviewed, we find a mild bias toward large programs. In our experience small scale projects can outperform large projects in terms of costs per unit of benefit. Economies of a large scale often disappear with overhead and coordination needs. The argument that problems are so large that only large programs are useful is often spurious. At times, it is simply a matter of having enough smaller projects to get the job done.

18. We are bemused by the number of supplicants that insist on believing that there is a "hidden agenda" of the grantor which, if known, will greatly increase the likelihood of funding. Our suggestion in these instances is that the investor whisper this response: "Psst...the real focus here is on results. The secret to getting funded is to state them clearly and forcefully."

19. Even when not in contradiction, resources can be redundant. For example, program transportation is often supported by the funding of vans or

buses that are dedicated to one program only. As a result, expensive vehicles that could handle half a dozen programs must sit idle much of the day while duplicate equipment makes the rounds for other programs.

20. Customers may choose not only among helpful options from a public perspective but unhelpful ones as well. A person may select to watch TV or take a nap rather than to solve a problem in *any* of the alternative ways offered.

21. Consider an investment in providing weekend respite to care givers of persons with disabilities where the outcome sought is reduced institutionalization of persons with a disability. The intensity question is clear: how many respite weekends does a family need to influence their decision on institutionalization? If research suggests that respite once every two months appears to be the lowest level that makes a difference, investors can assess the effectiveness of a stated performance target. If respite visits each cost $1,000. and an implementor requests $60,000, the investor would look for service to some 10 households, since this is the number that can be served with the minimum intensity needed. Respite to 20 families once every four months provides relief but no outcome.

22. While many organizations now speak fluently and proudly of their teams, most form teams in non-productive ways. They tend to celebrate similarities of members, for example, rather than to select for differences. See Williams, Harold S., "Entrepreneurial Team Building," ***INNOVATING***, Vol. 3, No. 4, Summer, 1993.

23. This guideline is an example of the criteria which, once stated, can become quality specifications for effective outcome funding systems. A requirement that all reports receive a personal response within 48 hours can make a substantial difference in anticipating and correcting problems. At the same time, it sets the pace for responsiveness by the implementor as well.

24. For a useful summary of recent thinking on this subject, Harry Hatry et al, editors, *Service Efforts and Accomplishments Reporting: Its Time Has Come*, Governmental Accounting Standards Board. Norwalk, Connecticut: 1990.

25. For a discussion of control and related issues at a structural level, see Williams, Harold S. "Taking the Middle Out of Management" in ***INNOVATING***, Vol. 2 No. 4, Summer, 1992.

26. In the private sector, the exit rate from the quality movement is now as high as the entrance rate. For a brief discussion of the problem areas in the public sector, see "Why Total Quality Management is Only Half a Loaf," Osborne, David, *Governing*, Aug. 1992.

27. Some high performing public sector organizations are setting aside their conventional "program development" models and focusing not on planning a *program* but on designing a *product*. The mind set is very different, involving, for example, the development of prototypes to test key assumptions during, rather than after design. See "Prototyping: When Planning Becomes Designing" by Marsters, Marsters E., and Williams, Harold S., ***INNOVATING***, Vol.3, No. 2, Winter, 1993.

28. Traditionally, the income (or profit/loss) statement is used only in the private sector. With increased efforts at revenue generation from public sector products, however, the income statement is an absolutely necessary tool for government. Our view is that applies even to mainstream services and operations whose only current revenue is a budget allocation.

29. Two reasons help to explain why Outcome Funding frequently encourages new groups. The first is that the new rules reduce the perceived advantage to incumbent grantgetters. Second, the more straightforward approach takes emphasis away from grantsmanship skills. No one takes off points for a misspelling in the target plan.

30. For an example of the comparison approach see: Semedei, Joseph and Williams, Harold S., *A Venture Capital Approach to Grant Making by Government... Case Study of a Teenage Prevention Program.* New York: The Rensselaerville Institute, 1987.

31. For further information, call or write to William J. Phillips, director of The Innovation Group, Rensselaerville, New York 12147.

PART III:

Targets & Accomplishments

The best reformers the world has ever seen are those who commence on themselves.

George Bernard Shaw

Chapter 12

Performance Targets and Outcomes

Picture the difference. Two teachers, Jim and Betty, each request $500 to try a new approach they believe will so engage their students that high truancy in their school will be reduced. Jim pledges to do his share to solve a school-wide problem by working hard to reduce absenteeism in all his classes. Betty states that she will focus on her second-period class where an average of 10 out of 32 students are not present. She indicates that her commitment is to do whatever it takes to reduce the absenteeism from 10 to five students.

If you had $500, in which teacher would you invest? In our framework, Betty is far more likely to produce the higher return. Why? Because she has a clear target on which to concentrate. Jim, in contrast, has no aiming point. His emphasis rests only on his activity.

Sanctifying Activity

In the grantmaking mindset, we fund activity, and activity is what we get. If a program seems in danger of not achieving its intended results, what most frequently happens? The end rather than the means is modified! If Jim's humanistic approach to education is not leading to increased attendance, then the likely explanation is that it is doing many other good things instead. If no one calls the 800-number for help, it must be that the advice in the public service message is self-explanatory. If people in a job-training program do not get and keep jobs, the real gain is that they have a higher sense of self-esteem. Funder often joins implementor in an ironic compact to hold the activity constant and let the results vary. One explanation for this turn of activity into stasis is that activities are for more familiar and tangible to most people than are outcomes. Activities are time-honored and sacred. They are, themselves, answers.

In the investment mode, priorities are reversed. The result stays constant and activities are allowed to vary. This can become a powerful means of breaking free from stereotypes. Consider the high school in which students were required to recite a key passage of the Bill of Rights. A teacher indicated that the reason sixty percent of his students did not know this passage was that they could not or would not memorize it. He believed a humanistic approach, including role-playing of the Founding Fathers, would lead to at least twenty of his students passing the test.

One week into his two-week initiative, the teacher saw virtually no change. Because he was so driven to get the students to recite the passage, the activity became suspect. The teacher awakened early one morning to a startling realization: the students *did* have the ability to memorize perfectly—if it was on their terms. In class that day, he told the students that he wanted them to "rap" the Bill of Rights. They could form groups and use music and instruments. The only rule was that they must use the exact words. At an assembly, the group with the best ability to communicate meaning in the "lyrics" would get a prize.

Almost all of the students learned the required passage—and had a clear sense of its meaning. If the desired result is held steady—whether memorizing the Bill of Rights, reducing teen pregnancy, increasing the speed of bridge repair, or anything else—we will much more readily question our course then if it is not. As the adage has it, if you don't know where you are going, any road will do.

Defining Performance Targets

Performance targets are literally the aiming points in Outcome Funding. They are more specific and delimited than formulations of goals and purposes, and they are free-standing, not qualified by motives or intents. Reaching them defines achievement for the program and return for the investor.

Performance targets are about change. By definition, they reflect a different reality than would have unfolded without a given intervention. Such change most often focuses on customers. Persons served by a program must literally intervene to modify or even turn around their own habits and routines.

Defining performance targets has two steps. The first is specifying the target areas. Thus an employment program may specify a focus on number of jobs created, how long the job lasts, and the cost per job created. The second step is to define a level of performance within each area. One program might define its target as the creation of *fifty* non-subsidized jobs that last at least six months at an implementor cost of no more than *$2,000* per job.

A common reaction from people in social and human services is that theirs is a "soft" area in which target specificity is simply not possible. How do you measure prevention? How do you quantify self-esteem? Others add that even if it is possible to specify target areas, it is impossible to specify levels. How do you know how many minority adoptions or pregnancy preventions are really possible or realistic? While these questions are noble, they miss the point. It is possible, as well as desirable, to define performance targets for virtually all programs funded by government. A case in point:

Apex Human Development (AHD) requested a grant roughly

equivalent to $50,000 to help deal with the awesome problem of teen pregnancy in their inner city. In the past, this group had indicated how many workshops it would hold for at-risk young women, and stressed the ways in which it built self-esteem as a preventive force. "Not sufficient," said their prospective financier, who uses the investor approach. "You are stating inputs, not results."

To respond, AHD narrowed its focus to two junior high schools and indicated it would work with twenty at-risk young women in each. Staff learned that, for young women with the particular characteristics of their customers, the pregnancy rate over the past three years had been 40%. They asked three persons, including the guidance counselor, to independently indicate their assessment of how many of the specific women with whom they would work were likely to get pregnant within the next eighteen months. In each case, the estimates proved close to the 40% statistical profile.

AHD people then indicated that it was their assumption that in each school, about eight of the twenty young women who they planned to include would get pregnant. They indicated their conviction that, as a result of their project, no more than four of these women would become pregnant.

The most important point from this example is that a baseline of present behavior is an important place to start. It lets the implementor determine a reasonable level of performance in the contexts of both specific customers and probably results. At the same time, it assures the investor that the project results are different from what would normally happen. (We have actually seen programs whose "achievements" were actually no better than what would have happened without the project!)

Note that the method for establishing a baseline need not

be expensive or complex. While not precise, the approach used here does use two independent sources of information (past statistics and personal forecasts), and indicates the target as an improvement on that baseline.

Performance targeting need not be simplistic, either. It simply asks that complexity be translated into tangible terms. Consider, for example, the question of quality. Many programs use this word in their mission statement. The purpose is to provide "quality day care," "quality counseling," and so on. Outcome Funding asks implementors to decide what quality means. If a group is distressed that its "quality jobs" are not distinguished from those of other groups supplying quantity jobs, they might make quality clear through such criteria as: a) a clear mobility path, such that designated performance will lead to at least a 10% pay increase within one year; b) health care coverage as part of reimbursement; c) employee preference, so that this job is within the top three job-area choices of the job holder.

Dimensions of Targets

A useful design principle is to shape products with an eye to their surroundings. A chair is crafted with a sense of the room in which it be placed, and a room's dimensions with knowledge of the home in which it exists. Performance targets also need a context—their customers.

One consequential factor is degree of difficulty in enabling or supporting a person to make a change. Some people are at a readiness threshold (in either motivational or skill terms) to use a park, say no to drugs, gain a job, or solve a pollution problem. A small nudge can make change happen for them. Others may require extensive and expensive support just to get to the starting line.

Such distinctions are important to make rational the level

of a performance target. Helping ten people with a second-grade education gain a high school equivalency may well be equal to helping one hundred people who have been through Grade 10. Context is also needed for the investor to understand the longer-term net effect of achieving a performance target. Here are some dimensions of potential interest:

> *Longevity effects.* A change which lasts for two weeks is obviously less useful than one which endures two years. Funding often ignores the time dimension, with the rationale that long-term tracking is too expensive. From a results focus, it can be an imperative. Without knowing long-term effects, short-term gains may or may not reflect an investment return. Often, the "quality" feature of a result is critical in enhancing longevity.[32]

> *Distributional effects.* How costs and benefits fall out (e.g., which customers succeed and which do not) can be a major concern to investors. In some investments, for example, fairness is measured not by equal access or allocation but by distribution of result.[33]

> *Side effects.* Some performance targets have a strong potential to create or to stimulate other effects. A new skill or capacity may well spill over to other arenas. In other cases, a gain in one area may prompt a loss in another. A person who begins to spend great time on community projects may do so at the cost of less time with his/her children.

Sources of Targets

Targets may originate in one of three places: the appropriator (who originates funds, often through a legislative process), the investor (who places the funds allocated), or the implementor. For the funder, the starting point is often policy. While policy formation is often taken to suggest a more generalized framework of goals and solutions, some governments have usefully demonstrated that government can begin with a performance accountability system at an overall level. As discussed in a useful new book called *Getting Results*, in the US, the state of Florida developed a sweeping but highly-specific Outcome focus on the state level in the 1980s. In the area of human service, their framework for limiting institutions is as follows: [34]

- Reduce the patient population by 413 to a total of 2,769 in the four major state mental hospitals by June 30, 1984, through the expansion of community alternatives, and increase Community Care for the Elderly core services from 20,215 to 23,674 served, which will serve 14% of the identified need.

The same framework was applied to transportation and the outcomes of safe and efficient travel:

- Resurface 1,600 lane miles (reduce the deficiency backlog from 7,400 to 7,000 miles by July 1, 1984), and maintain 34,350 land miles (including 5,450 on the interstate system) at overall service level of 70% of full maintenance standards.

These statements provide a clear outcome-oriented framework for those agencies to which funds are allocated.

In complex problems, a government-wide performance target may well lead to quite different means from specific agencies which invest. If a mayor sets the target of reducing the number of homeless on the streets from 5,000 to 2,000 persons, the Mental Health Department would look for treatment strategies, the Housing Agency would increase the supply of low-income homes, the Economic

Development Agency would seek to create new jobs for homeless people.

In such a case, government as a whole may wish to make assumptions about what kinds of products will best lead to customer use and results, and allocate monies accordingly. In this instance, it is assuming an investor function of selectivity. Alternatively, the mayor, legislator, or governor may supply many agencies with funds and let each make its own decisions about targeting. A drawback of this approach in that each agency will "lobby its hobby" and tend to see a significant portion of the homeless as needing that agency's services.

While policy and programmatic accountability systems may be formed on a federal, state, or city-wide basis, the more likely profile is targeting by specific agencies which will invest monies. In these instances, the investor will typically state the areas of performance targets as a given. Where possible, we urge the investor to also indicate area-wide target levels sought. Each applicant can then indicate what portion of that target they are prepared to assume. Differentiation of customers will again be used to make a specific achievement rational.

While investors may resist this level of specificity as curtailing the creativity of the implementing groups, our experience is that it does not. Indeed, clear boundaries and givens often enhance creativity by concentrating it. In the Outcome framework, the approach and activities employed to get to the result are entirely in the hands of the implementor.

At times, the palette for applicants can be broader. If the investor either does not know what performance targets will best achieve an outcome or wishes to support multiple targets as determined by those seeking money, it can ask the implementor to define the result. In that case, the definition of both area and level of performance target vests with the grant-seeker.

Whatever the source of performance targets, the important point is that both investor and implementor must agree to them in advance of the investment decision. We do not suggest, however, that targets necessarily be developed in a collaborative way. In particular, no implementor should feel a reduced obligation to achieve a performance target on the grounds that someone else helped develop them!

The Units of Service Fallacy

Many funders believe they are achieving rigor by quantifying service. By using the common denominator of costs per hour of training, counseling, or other service, they point with pride to their ability to compare proposers and achieve cost-effective programs.

In the outcome framework, units of service are units of activity, not of result, and the cheapest price may prove the most costly. Funders of training programs, for example, may be pleased to achieve a cost of no more than $100 per trainee day. If they are getting a second-rate trainer who has no ability to relate content to the circumstances of those present, however, the money may be wasted. A cost of $300 per day may be far more effective if it buys a brilliant trainer whose teachings prompt strong outcomes.

Another qualifier is an understanding of the total costs of a function. For example, investors in meetings who focus exclusively on the charge rate of the speaker are actually dealing with the smallest part of expense. Participant time is the major cost. In this context, adding $500 to get a better speaker may leverage gains for the $5,000 or more of staff time invested. [35]

Many people mistakenly see the outcome approach as substituting quantity for quality. In reality, the shift more often goes in the opposite direction. In the above example, the *quality* of the trainer is far more relevant than the *quantity* of his or her daily fee.

Unit of service-thinking can lead to the wrong conclusion in large as well as small programs. Consider this example:

When co-author Arthur Webb became director of the drug-response agency in New York State, he was told that residential treatment for drug-dependent persons was the key program funded, and that the cost per day of treatment ranged from the equivalent of $50 to $100, depending on area of state and degree of client problems. The agency was buying a person in a bed with a prescribed set of services, carefully regulated and monitored. This director was not satisfied with the unit cost approach, and asked what was known of the results of residential treatment. An important fact soon surfaced. If people remained in the beds until they graduated from a full-treatment sequence, the likelihood of long-term reduced use of drugs was significantly increased. If they left before completion, no long-term gain could be anticipated.

The director also learned that on the average, five persons entered and left a residential treatment bed before one remained through a full-treatment program. He then decided that it made no sense to buy daily services for a person in a bed. The lowest unit of useful purchase for this investor was completion of treatment.

Two implications come from this example.

1. *Unit costs are not always what they seem.* If a treatment sequence takes 400 days at an average daily cost of $100, the cost for a treatment program is *$40,000* per person. If the five persons who did not

stay through to graduation collectively occupied that same bed for a total of 200 days, the true cost for each graduation achieved is actually *$60,000*. The point is to load costs onto results, not activities.

2. *Unit costing can lead to the wrong strategy.* In this case, the strategy of adding new beds is actually less effective than making more effective the beds that already exist. Why spend $15,000 or more in capital costs to create beds that in five of six cases at any point in time are not leading to a gain?

The Delivery System Paradigm

The public sector has a label that describes many of the activities it conducts and funds others to perform. "Delivery system" as a mindset explains why units of service are held in such high esteem. An example is the social service delivery system. It assumes the presence of a premade *service* that is delivered to *clients* as part of a *system*. Whatever the program, it need only be administered in the right dosages to ensure success for interchangeable customers. The focus is on the behavior of the provider. The client may—and indeed should—remain patient and passive until his or her medicine arrives. The same imagery and expectations about responsibility and initiative apply to other expressions, including "safety net." [36]

In the delivery system paradigm, productivity means number of units of service delivery, and efficiency means low cost. Management means coordination of system elements, and accountability means delivering the service in a correct and uniform matter. Evaluation determines if all of this is done.

In the delivery system framework, what is given is presumed equivalent to what is received, and what is received is equal to what is used. Use is then equated to gain. The fragility in these equations is self-evident.

On Performance Contracting

Performance contracting is a prominent example of the Outcome Funding approach. It ties performance to payment. In some cases, payments are contingent on achieving a specified result. In others, a lower fixed fee is augmented by a bonus offered for higher-than-predicted performance. While relatively new to government, derivatives of performance contracting have been in place for over a century in business. For example, a retainer is kept by the buyer until all work is completed, and a penalty in dollars-per-day is imposed for late completion. More broadly, companies are moving from payment-for-time to payment-for-production. Thirty percent of the Fortune 500 companies are now experimenting with some form of pay-for-performance program that involves some four million workers. [37]

In performance-based contracting, the key question is what performance means. When the approach defines fulfillment as units of service, it is simply a more rigorous application of input-oriented funding. In other cases, it overly simplifies investment by equating it to procurement—literally the "buying" of something. Investors want a return, not a commodity. Still, the straightforward concept of paying when and if results occur is both attractive and instructive. In particular, this logical end point of Outcome Funding raises two common objections, to which we find useful responses.

#1: *Performance contracting leads to "creaming."* The concern is that those most readily brought to the desired outcome will be served, and those most resistant or difficult will be ignored. We have two answers. First, if the initial people assisted are those with the least severe problem and moving them out permits better focus on those with more severe problems, isn't this useful? If we simply debate the matter of who to serve first, no one gets help.

More importantly, if counterproductive or inequitable selection of customers takes place, the investor more than the implementor is at fault. The investor can differentiate any kinds of customers. Different payment levels can create strong incentives to deal with any given level of difficulty.

In this sense, performance contracting is a good tool for shifting the traditional focus on levels of need to a more productive look at levels of result. That is, a given level of program intervention may well achieve different gains for different people.

#2: *Performance contracting reduces complex outcomes to simplistic measures.* What is rewarded is what will be done. What is on the test is what will be taught. This is certainly a reality. The response, however, is not to retreat from investment rigor, but to vigorously pursue effective definition. If a school determines, for example, that it will reward the learning of analytical and problem-solving skills rather than memorization, it can and will find a way to define these gains, and then teach and test to that target.

The "And Then" Connector

Our picture is of a sequence of activities leading to performance targets. Parts of these elements may also be seen as a chain or progression. A group implementing a project desired to get fifty women to visit a prenatal clinic and follow the advice given them might well use the "and then" connector in this way.

The starting point: a core activity.

> First we will design, print, and mail brochures to 5,000 women who are pregnant or likely to become so.

And then?

> Some of the women who get the brochure will choose to read it and call one of the clinics listed.

And then?

> Some of the women who call the clinic will both make an appointment to visit and will keep that appointment.

A final "And then?" gets us to the performance target:

> Some of the women who visit the clinic will carefully follow the nutritional and other advice given them.

At this point, the connector leads us to an outcome—the end state desired by investors:

> Those women who follow advice will have children with higher birth weights and reduced infant mortality.

The connecting question becomes a *locational device*, ensuring that implementors know where they are in the chain. In the above example, how many implementors—and funders—stop at the very first activity of printing and mailing the brochure, blissfully unaware that they are only on the first step?

Targets as Motivators

We have suggested in earlier chapters that the real point of having targets is not to allow for evaluation but to boost performance. This process happens in several ways.

When we say that people with a target outperform those

without one, we are, in part, talking about the power of expectations. It is an extraordinary shaper of behavior. Experiments in education, for example, show that if teachers are informed that certain students have great potential, they will, in fact, learn more or learn faster than students with the same abilities who are not so designated. Prophecies tend to be self-fulfilling—but only if those involved are aware of them. [38]

Targets are also useful in influencing customer behavior. A strategy of many implementors is to share the target with their customers and ask for their help in reaching it. "I'm desperate, kids. For me to succeed in this project, I must find a way to get five more of you coming to class each day. What will it take to get you to do that?" This method of spreading responsibility is seen in such practices as the barometer sign in United Fund drives. The feedback on how much money has been raised is not, by itself, motivating. It is the portrayal of current dollars contributed vs. the goal which counts.

For implementors and, occasionally, their customers, targets define success. They are the equivalents of the score in a basketball game, a gain or loss in the stock market. For some persons, targets are not overly important in life. For others, they are critical and even compelling. The motivation may be externally competitive—to do better that another person or another group. It may be internal—to achieve a target set regardless of whether anyone else even knows about it.

David McClelland's research on achievement motivation suggests that achievement can be as important a human drive as the need for approval and belonging or the need for power or efficacy. [39] Achievement motivation is not possible without a target. When some persons and proposing groups resist the setting of performance targets—especially ambitious ones—this is an important indicator for the investor.

On the Nature of Outcomes

If performance targets are very different from activities, so too, are outcomes distinct from performance targets. Targets are the end points for activities, whereas outcomes are the end points for targets. In general, targets help to implement while outcomes specify the job of the investor.

Outcomes express end-states which are considered sufficient for resolving a problem or grasping an opportunity. Generally, they are expressed not in the terms of individual gains for customers which characterize performance targets, but as collective gains for those with problems and those who would help them. One example would be a community or a nation with no unpreventable infant mortality. A school to which all students wish to go on every school day is another.

In some cases, outcomes and performance targets may overlap or even prove identical. Achievement of a high school equivalency for some investors may be the final outcome. In most cases, however, that achievement is seen as a means to a broader end—whether employment, reduced recidivism for those on parole, prevention of drug abuse or anything else.

The distinction between performance targets and outcomes challenges some conventional assumptions. For example, most of us, when asked why people sign up for dieting programs would answer, "To lose weight." But this is seldom the real goal. It is not high weight in itself that is the problem, but other conditions that are presumed associated with weight. In reality, the outcome sought is better health, greater attractiveness to others, higher feelings of worth. "Pounds off" is the performance target which is connected to the outcome.

Targets represent minimal accomplishments which implementors believe they can "pull off" given the factors they can control or finesse. Outcomes often include factors beyond the control of individual implementors. Indeed, a number of investments, each leading to specified performance targets, may be necessary for an outcome to be achieved.

Outcomes reflect visions—lie considerably beyond present reality. The only requirement for an outcome is that investors must be able to state it clearly and compellingly, and to define the ways in which specific project returns will lead to or even cause its attainment. Again, that is the investors' responsibility, not the implementors'.

Connecting Targets to Outcomes

The focus on performance targets pries us free from the activity trap, but leaves us vulnerable to the next connection: between target and outcome. Simply put, how do we know that the target is meaningful? Consider the large case of prevention. Many public sector funds support groups which deal in the prevention of drug abuse, teen pregnancy, and many other problems. A common activity is the distribution of information—facts and figures galore about the problem and its implications.

In response to increased public scrutiny about what is realized from media campaigns, flyers, classroom training, and other modes of dissemination, many information-based prevention programs have moved toward performance targets. The most common is a focus on information gained and retained. Through a pre- and post-test, implementors ensure that a certain percentage of those exposed to facts remember them. In a few cases, they also measure retention at a later point.

This is a clear performance target, but it is often not a good one. Research in drug abuse and other fields is increasingly clear that information alone—even if retained—is rarely enough to change behavior! [40] If the desired outcome of prevention is reduced abuse of drugs, then achieving retention—the performance target—is not sufficient (or, in some cases, even necessary) to bring it about. While the implementor's focus is on his or her performance target, the investor's first focus is on ensuring that the achievement of targets has a relationship to achieving outcomes.

In many instances, research and/or documented practice has shown a relationship between target and outcome, at least on a statistical basis in large populations. Here are some examples:

Target	Outcome
less truancy	higher test scores
reduced weight	better health
more visits to pre-natal clinics	lower infant mortality
more teen jobs	fewer teen pregnancies

In many instances, however, the connection is either not present or in dispute. Educators, for example, do not agree that higher test scores are connected to the outcome of higher reasoning skills.

The Outcome Shuffle

Just as performance targets can be too readily altered, so too, can outcomes. In one large state, regional newspapers began to carry stories of possible closure of a college campus within a statewide public education system. In their vigorous defense of keeping the school open, its administrators—with no objection from the system's leadership—stressed one key reason for keeping the school alive: preserving jobs in a poor county. No one referred to an educational rationale.

While the political astuteness of the response is admirable, the mixing of motives by investors is not. Indeed, if a campus or any other public facility has economic vitality as its desired outcome, then 50% of its budget should be covered by that state's economic development agency!

Outcome instability can also happen in more overt form. Prisons and even drug treatment centers, for example, walk a tightrope between the outcome of keeping dangerous or undesirable people off the streets and rehabilitating inmates and patients. The performance targets for these outcomes are very different, as are the activities designed to bring them about.

Another derivative of this problem is seen in the contrast between the outcomes of staying afloat and remaining on course. When organizations funded by government spend over 50% of the monies they earn on the costs of raising it, survival as an outcome is equally important as service and direction. When a group which solves one problem quickly pounces on another to avoid its own extinction, the same condition—called goal reversal— prevails. The means becomes the end. [41]

Watching the Words

Our work on Outcome Funding since the first edition of this book has taught us the power of words. The diction we use clearly conditions our thinking. Given that we want new thinking, we suggest your indulgence with our terminology, especially in the outcome arena.

Many people speak of goals as broad end states and objectives as more specific means to achieve them. We much prefer Outcomes and Performance Targets. A "goal" is a nebulous creature. It may be an aspiration, a mission, a purpose, a value, or a preferred condition. And the term "objective" is often used to include many forms of input, as in the expression, "process objective." In general, goals and objectives are often used to signify intent and purpose. We prefer direction and commitment to a destination.

Another term in the common parlance is result. It is a hard word to avoid, as you will see for its inadvertent use in this book. The problem is that when we ask "What are your results?" we are asking for what happened. We can only learn this after the fact. Our approach asks for performance targets to be set in advance with verification used to learn if targets have been hit.

Chapter 13

Milestones and Milestones Management

The eager chief executive of a new business is in town to report progress to his investor. His rationale to his investor:

> Six months ago, you gave me my first $500,000 to start this business. I am pleased to report that I spent all the money you gave me in a responsible and legal way. I found office space, hired people, added great new features to my product, engaged an ad agency, and developed a strategic plan. My expense documentation is excellent. Now, please give me a second $500,000.

Given this report, the financing agent would be very reluctant to advance another dime. There is no evidence presented that the business will work. Yet, funding agencies routinely advance more funds on the criteria that an activities checklist is complete, and that the implementor has spent all the money previously advanced!

In business, the implementing group tracks not activities but milestones, defined as those critical interim points that assure everyone that the program will achieve its performance target. Milestones are constructed to get a positive response to three questions:

1. *Will anybody want to buy and make use of this product?* (Often it turns out that only the maker is highly enthusiastic about what he/she produces!)

2. *Can we make this product within prescribed cost*

and quality guidelines? (Often unforeseen expenses emerge and economies of scale prove elusive.)

3. *Are there enough people out there who want this?* (When a venture runs out of its friends, sales can plateau well beneath a break-even volume.)

Programs financed by government will find these questions just as relevant as for-profit firms. Consider the "one church-one child" model of adoption pioneered by Father Clements in Illinois and now financed in other states. Non-profit groups using this approach seek black and Hispanic churches which will persuade one or more of their members to adopt a minority child. For this program, questions might translate as follows.

1. *Can I find one minority church which will agree to place a child and then do so?*

   Programs attempting to offer public services are often top-heavy with early planning and the development of needed infrastructure—staff, space, manuals, and so on. In a surprising number of cases, errors show up in the inferences made about what will happen once the program begins. Prominent among these is the tenet that customers really want the product. In this case, potential churches may well say yes to the hypothetical question, "Would you be interested in working with us to place a minority child in foster care in the adoptive home of one of your parishioners?" When it's time to perform, the answer may be no.

   Even when pre-project indicators are encouraging, the minister may not accurately estimate the disposition of church members to take up this challenge. In virtually any marketing context, the contrast between those seriously interested and those who can and will buy is significant. If the expectation of early customers (who are critical in leading by example) breaks down, the project will crash quickly. For this reason, it is imperative that an early milestone be the securing of an actual customer. Note that this means not simply finding one church, but an adoptive household within it.

2. *Can we control costs and quality over the complete time and range of our program?*

Although their form may be different, public service programs face the same "production" issues as do private businesses. A common program is to underestimate just what can be done in a day or a month. In this example, the implementor might project that a person can make visits to six churches in a day and base the performance target on that belief. The organization then finds that staff time spent waiting for phone calls, subways, approvals, or meetings reduces this level to four daily visits. The performance target is in jeopardy.

Costs may also prove higher than anticipated. Prices of airfares or supplies may increase beyond projection, as may quantities. Indeed, cost overruns on social and human services are as prevalent in our experience as are overruns on most other kinds of contracts. They are simply less obvious, since the tendency is to reduce results as an adjustment. Expectations are downsized. [42]

Quality problems are equally probable. A common one is that people with the right skills cannot be found for the salaries offered. Either much time is spent in hiring and rehiring due to rapid turnover, or people who are hired cannot represent the full quality of the program in those many instances when they alone must express it.

3. *Are there enough churches and church members who will work with us to achieve our target?*

Four to five people who sell life insurance on a commission basis leave within a year. The most common reason: they run out of friends. When the "cold" calls start, success rates can plummet. Whether seeking churches for adoption or schools for a new prevention program, the same problem can occur. Many programs mistakenly place their customer expectations on groups and people who have a special reason to be interested, but who are not of sufficient number to provide all needed customers.

Readiness is one reason why the last customer is harder to find than the second. Most programs define their market niche through pre-qualifications. [43] In the adoption project, once the first people are aboard, it may that a very low percentage of those interested can meet the rigorous home study or other criteria required for child placement. An additional problem is that programs can confuse need with demand. The key is not how many people the implementor sees as needing his or her wares, but the number of people who see themselves as wanting to use them.

Customer Steps vs. Implementor Steps

The most useful aspect of most management approaches is that they provide focus. From mission statements to management by objectives, to total quality management, the point is to have an efficient way of sifting through the constant barrage of reports and meetings, budgets and statistics, to decide what is most important. By telling you what to *include*, management tools give you the permission to also *exclude*. Selectivity of action is a core strength of high-performing managers.

Traditionally, accountability focuses on the workplan implementors do. For example, a program seeking to provide job training workshops and placement for persons currently unemployed might be defined by this abbreviated sequence of tasks:

A. *Preparations Phase*

1. Develop a list of potential participants and mail program announcement to everyone on that list.

2. Hold information meeting for those interested and identify participants.

3. Prepare all workshop content.

4. Define potential job placement sites.

B. *Implementation Phase*

1. Conduct all courses.

2. Place workshop graduates in a job-training position.

3. Provide follow-up support to people while on the jobs.

The problem with both implementor and investor focus on

this workplan is that it is perfectly possible to go through these eight steps and conclude with a well-documented failure. The reason is this incongruity: activity focuses on what the implementor does, while the performance target hinges on what the customer does. Milestones suggest starting with all essential steps that define a participant's interaction with a program on the way to a successful result. For the above example, the program from the participant's perspective might look as follows:

Participants:

1. Learn of program.
2. Decide to enroll.
3. Attend first session.
4. Retain information/skills from first session.
5. Attend all remaining sessions.
6. Retain information/skills from all sessions.
7. Start at job site.
8. Performs satisfactorily on job.
9. Stay at this for at least six months.

This progression includes all of the separable steps that must be achieved in the customer-through-program sequence. For example, unless the people retain the information from the first session, it does not matter if they attend all remaining sessions. They have left the trail to performance target, which presumes that they need to retain workshop content to get to sustained employment.

The core focus for any program is the passage of customers through milestones. But the question is more specific: Are *enough* people arriving at each step to ensure the number of customers who are to get to a result? In the above program, for example, let's assume that the implementor has told the investor in their target plan that they will deliver a result of fifty persons getting and keeping a job for six months. That's the performance target. With this end point established, the milestone question becomes, "How many people do we need at each milestone building to the point of fifty people who get and keep a job?"

Here is the response to this question of the job training example:

MILESTONE	NUMBER NEEDED
1. Learn of project	2,000
2. Decide to enroll	400
3. Attend first session	300
4. Retain information/skills from first session	200
5. Attend all remaining sessions	100
6. Retain information/skills from all sessions	100
7. Start at job site	80
8. Perform satisfactorily on job	60
9. Stay at job for at least six months	50

We can now take the final step in the customer milestones by adding conversion factors. These factors literally tell us how many people "convert" from one step to the next. In the insurance business, for example, salespeople believe that it takes one hundred "cold" calls to get ten meetings scheduled and that it takes ten meetings to gain one sale. Therefore, if sales agents want or need to make ten sales, they would be well served by starting with a thousand calls. Here are the conversions for our job placement illustration. Note that each factor is established by dividing the lower milestone step number into the higher one. Thus, four hundred divided into two thousand yields a conversion factor of five from step # 1 to step # 2. Also note that we are now graphically depicting customer steps as a funnel. More people go in at the top than come out the bottom with a result.

MILESTONES	NUMBER NEEDED	CONVERSION FACTOR
1. Learn of project	2,000	
2. Decide to enroll	400	5.0
3. Attend first session	300	1.3
4. Retain information/skills from first session	200	1.5
5. Attend all remaining sessions	100	2.0
6. Retains information/ skills from all sessions	100	1.0
7. Start at job site	80	1.2
8. Performs satisfactorily on job	60	1.3
9. Stay at job for at least 6 months	50	1.2

If you have the numbers, why worry about conversion factors? There are two reasons. The first is that the factors are a splendid piece of shorthand for looking at program efficiency. They tell you not only how many people are dropping out of your funnel, but at what points. One is the perfect number in this framework. It reflects a one hundred percent conversion; no one has left the result track. While higher numbers are inevitable, you can work not only to reduce them, but to strategically place them. A high fall-out rate in an early step, for example, is generally far less costly than at a later step, where monies have been used to get a customer toward the end of your funnel. Second, many programs are phased such that total numbers do not materialize until late in the program. Assume that in our job placement example the plan is to hold three series of workshops over a year. In the opening quarter, a first mailing of two hundred brochures leads to twenty people who enroll and ten persons who actually show up for the first session. It is the conversion factors—not the numbers—that tell us that this program is in trouble. The anticipated conversions from two hundred people informed would be forty people enrolled and thirty people attending the first course.

The numbers used in the above charts are purely hypothetical. In ongoing programs, the experience base provides the numbers for each milestone and the conversion factor needed at each milestone can be closely approximated. However, for new programs, this will not be true. The implementor may have to begin with a "best-guess" estimate. This is acceptable and far better than having no logical starting pint at all. Also, if there is no direct experience base, more generalized behavior can be used in creating the program. For example, there are generally know ratios for people who call a "hotline" telephone number after receiving a brochure or watching a television show. The given program may be different from that for which the ratios were determined, but the generic behavior provides a rough baseline which may be used by the implementor. After one year's experience, one can then refine the numbers and the conversion factors to become much more accurate.

For a new program, another good way to start is to arbitrarily choose a starting number of customers to go through the funnel. By working through the funnel, one can determine conversion factors for each milestone. One would then determine the performance target to be achieved, or, in other words, the end number of people that you want to go through the customer funnel. Working up through the funnel using the conversion factors one has determined with the hypothetical model, allows one to then determine the real numbers of customers one needs to begin the milestone program.

Dealbreakers

If customers are to progress to the target as projected, several factors need a watchful eye because they may prove to be "dealbreakers." The first is intermediaries.

Intermediaries are those actors or forces upon whom you are depending upon to play a critical role and whom you do not directly control. For example, a program on preventing drug abuse may hinge on the willingness of a school to allow the project into its classrooms. The intermediary focus is not only on the school whose help is needed, but on the key decision-makers within that school.

Many prevention programs rely on support from principals and superintendents that they welcome a preventive program, for example, only to find that when the time comes for implementation, classroom teachers do not cooperate. Intermediaries are usefully seen as customers. If you do not meet their needs, you cannot get to your "end-users."

Moreover, what the teachers need to be cooperative may be different from what the students need to avoid drug abuse, and it may also be different from what administrators want. While the principal is looking to gain good public relations, the classroom teacher wants to buy only those programs which will save them time or produce simplicity in a world growing more burdensome and complex.

Intermediaries tend to come in three categories. *Service actors*—including classroom teachers in the above example—are people or groups on whom you rely for direct project actions. *Approval actors* are those you need for some type of permit or permission. A program placing children for adoption, for example, relies on a local social service agency to approve the home studies of the adopting families. *Resource actors* are those needed to supply money, equipment, volunteers or some other needed element on which the program is dependent. An agency relied upon for customer referrals is an example.

The milestone format asks that intermediaries be identified in advance, along with their evidence of anticipated commitment. Tracking then takes place to ensure that commitments and actions materialize as projected. Again, the milestone focus is desired to let you see problems at an early point.

Money as a Dealbreaker

Financial accountability in most programs is limited to monitoring by line-item expense. From a results focus, this is of little value. The meaningful question is whether the money is going to last to accomplish customer progress through all milestones. In Chapter 7, we discussed the notion of costs per unit of result. In the milestone framework, we refine this to cost per milestone. Let's use as an example the job training project already identified.

Assume that the total budget is $100,000. Given fifty people achieving the job target, we know that the overall cost is $2,000 per customer. The more useful question is what will it cost to reach each of the nine customer step milestones. After calculations, this program might offer the following breakdown:

CUSTOMER MILESTONES	STAFF COSTS($)	OTHER COSTS ($)	TOTAL ($)	COST PER CUSTOMER
1. 2,000 people learn of project	5,800	2,000	7,800	3.90
2. 400 decide to enroll	6,000	1,000	7,000	17.50
3. 300 attend first session	6,000	600	6,600	22.00
4. 200 retain information/skills from 1st session	12,000	600	12,600	63.00
5. 100 attend all sessions	20,600	800	21,400	214.00
6. 100 retain information/skills from all sessions	10,000	600	10,600	106.00
7. 80 start job	10,000	800	10,800	135.00
8. 60 perform job satisfactorily	16,000	600	16,600	277.00
9. 50 stay on job six months	6,000	600	6,600	132.00
TOTALS:	92,400	7,600	100,000	

Monitoring the money in this way asks the implementor to again track the difference between projections and reality. The cost per person is needed for the same reason that the conversion factor is necessary. It allows everyone to see if experience is consistent with expectation at an early point. If a project is spending more money than intended to get its first customers to attend and to learn from early sessions, the best prediction is that this will happen for the remainder of the customers. The result: not enough money is left to handle remaining steps. Also, it is another way of looking at efficiencies. High per-person costs at an early point are generally to be avoided.

The projecting and tracking of costs by function is called cost accounting—literally a distribution or loading of expenses to critical parts of the enterprise. A detailed explanation of this approach and how to use it in a public service environment will be contained in the companion volume to *Outcome Funding* called *Outcome Finance*, to be published by The Rensselaerville Institute in late 1994.

Examples of Other Dealbreakers

Performance on customer milestones and the two key dealbreakers—money and intermediaries—are tracked by a comparison between projections and experience. Some additional factors are equally critical but better stated with a simple "yes or no" format. In general, they are factors that will not cause a problem unless a shift or change takes place. Among the factors in this category:

- That customers continue to reflect those individuals or groups the implementor is contracted to serve. This assurance is to avoid the possibility of programs shifting customers (often toward those more readily available or more easily brought to a result) once underway.

- That the same key individuals profiled in the target plan continue in place and with no question of their capability or performance status. This assurance is anchored in the premise that the persons are as important as the plan. The investors need to know if there is any likelihood of a key person leaving the program and, if so, who will replace them.

- That nothing has shifted in the environment which would have an adverse effect on achieving the

> performance target. This assures the investor that the implementor is scanning their environment to see if some kind of economic, institutional, or other change is taking place that would have an impact on its results. An employment program, for example, which suddenly learns of a large plant closing in their small city, is most likely in jeopardy.

Implementors are often asked to sign contracts or agreements to ensure that these factors are considered. They are stating that, to the best of their knowledge, no changes concerning customers, key people, or environmental shifts have occurred or are anticipated. Programs may well have additional factors.

Management by Milestones

> With the milestones, we have set a target for ourselves that we are to complete. This keeps us on schedule and acts as a focal point. We work on the task for a while, letting it sail along. At a given point, we stop to see if what we are doing is getting us to that target. If it is not, we re-evaluate and do something else. I always found myself changing my method in order to achieve milestones. [44]

These comments from the project director of a non-profit group using Outcome Funding underscore the management value of the milestone tool. The notion of changing activities to reach a target is clearly at work. Milestones set priorities.

Course correcting

Milestones do not prevent people from drifting off course. Rather, they are a way of discovering drift at an early point—when there is still time to do something about it. In social programs, as in medicine, most problems are correctable only if detected and treated while they remain small and formulative, rather than large and entrenched.

When customer milestone projections are not being reached, which may involve problems with intermediaries or money, the implementor has a limited set of options to consider. They are:

1. *Change customers.* Within the market a program is committed to serve, it may have the right product for the wrong customers. If one size does not cover all, perhaps the problem is one of fit. This option generally applies best to the early end of the customer funnel, where inferences about why people will want to participate in a program may prove inaccurate.

2. *Change product quantities.* If customers are entering the program but not getting to results, the problem may not be the customers *or* the product but rather the intensity and duration of the connection between them. Evaluation research suggests that many programs are doing the right thing—but just not enough of it with each customer to ensure the result sought.

3. *Change product qualities.* Another option is change in a core feature of the program design. A television campaign on child abuse, for example, might have assumed that the best way to get people to seek help is to scare them. Hence, the early pictures are filled with abused children and threats about going to prison. The implementor may learn that for their viewing audience, the carrot is more compelling than the stick. Hence a change in core characteristic from avoiding the adverse to embracing the positive (e.g., images of healthy, happy households) may be

in order.

4. *Change the delivery agents.* With most services, the product is not separable from its delivery. Perhaps it is the style or approach of the people who connect customers with products that need adjustment. People are not overly malleable. For example, if participants need a workshop leader who can definitely answer their questions rather than refer them to others, it is often better to find a new person than try to transform a cautious educator into a decisive one. Or vice versa.

5. *Change the milestone.* When all else fails, look here. Perhaps the milestone projection itself was in error. The implementor may discover that while they projected needing 500 persons at milestone 3 to get to 300 at milestone 5, they now think that having 400 people at milestone 3 is sufficient. The real issue with changes in milestones, of course, is whether the performance target must also be modified.

Implementors assessing these options must, as a starting point, list their core assumptions for each potential change. What did they most assume to be true of customers, of program intensity and features, and of effective delivery agent characteristics? The chances are excellent that one or more of these assumptions has broken down. Wherever assumptions fall short, this is the most likely change arena for making a course correction.

Renee Avery, executive director of another non-profit group using milestones, talks about the implications of this kind of focus in terms of the impact on program accountability:

> The milestones method definitely made us more accountable, which, from a programmatic perspective, was a plus. The director of the project was required to make a basic decision either to become accountable to results or to get out of the business of foster placement. [45]

This group, incidentally, worked on the problem of recruiting foster homes for babies in hospitals whose families could not have them at home. Their performance target was fifteen placements. With the use of milestones, they achieved forty-six.

A key advantage of milestone management is simplicity. While a work plan for three months might consume five to ten pages, most quarterly milestones fit on one page. As high performing organizations have known for some time, when it comes to objectives, less is usually more. The complexity and abstraction of most plans and mission statements is one reason they remain in drawers more than in minds.

Accelerated Prototyping

Private sector companies developing new products use a technique called rapid aging. They will put a new paint, for example, in an environmental chamber to simulate ten years of weather in sixty days. They do so to anticipate longer term effects on such characteristics as adhesion, chalking, mildew, and color change. Public service programs can use a similar technique called accelerated prototyping. Prototypes are early uses of a product and are increasingly favored over long planning cycles. Their value is to test key assumptions that in the normal cycle of events would not surface until a later moment, when change is difficult and very expensive.

In our context, accelerated prototyping means running a few

customers through all of the milestones at an early moment. This not only looks quickly and closely at conversion factors but at intermediaries, cost per step, and checklist factors as well. Do staff and intermediaries do everything they anticipated doing? Do conversions hold? While answers based on a few early return are not final proof, they go a long way toward providing reassurances and suggesting course corrections.

Milestones are far more than an additional accountability step. As with other tools in this book, their power lies not in monitoring or measuring performance, but in improving it. Performance targets provide the rationale for course corrections. Milestones provide the means.

Chapter 14

Verifying Accomplishments

At the end of a project, how does the funder know if he or she has achieved a return? The common answer: evaluation. This prescription is soothing to the grant maker in its focus on documentation and accountability. But it may not be the right medicine for either investors or the projects which they support.

Evaluation in Perspective

While evaluation serves important purposes, from the investor's perspective it is as likely to hinder performance as help it. Consider seven distinctions.

1. *Explanations vs. accomplishment.* In their search for understanding, many evaluations give great weight to reasons. A well-explained failure may earn higher marks than a tersely reported success. From the investor's perspective, there is a thin line between an explanation (no matter how profound) and an excuse. Reasons are not readily confused with results. Further, they can achieve substantial gain without knowing precisely why something works as well as it does. It is not that understanding is unimportant, but that it is not the highest priority goal for most investments. (Innovation investments are an exception, as discussed in Chapter 17.)

2. *Focus on implementors vs. focus on customers.* Traditional evaluations focus on treatments. They assume that the program plan and accuracy in its delivering are the keys to success. In the investment

approach, explanations for success or failure are more likely to lie in the way a customer responds to a program. User-based factors are as relevant as program-based factors.

3. *Documenting change vs. verifying targets.* Evaluations seek to define levels of impact. They can proceed as readily in the absence of targets as in their presence. Investors require a target for measurement to have meaning. Unanticipated effects—even beneficial ones—are much less relevant, but perhaps equally important to recognize.

4. *Objective measurement vs. biased success.* Evaluators often require that a program be implemented without change so that its assumptions or theories can be tested in a reasonably pure manner. In contrast, investors not only allow but encourage course corrections. They literally do everything possible to bias a program toward success.

5. *Population vs. sample.* Evaluators often view program participants as a sample drawn from a complete universe of people with a certain need or problem. They wish to understand the degree to which the sample is representative of that larger group. For many investors, the sample is the universe. If a project is focused on helping 100 persons get a job, the investor's interest is on what happens to those 100 persons, not the additional 10,000 people who are unemployed in that particular city.

6. *Predictable vs. idiosyncratic factors.* Evaluations seek to define "lawful" effects which are relatively consistent over time. This is presumed to enable replication of treatments which work. Investors tend to put as much stock in energetic and even

unpredictable individuals as in program templates. They wish to buy present value more than future prospects.

7. *Deferred precision vs. present approximation.* Evaluations seek accuracy. Conclusions often depend on differences that prove statistically significant, with findings set forth in formal documents. From the investor's perspective, close approximations which are immediately and informally available are often more useful than precise measurements available in six months.

Beyond its different purposes, evaluation may hold deeper issues from an investor perspective. Alice Rivlin of the Brookings Institute offers this musing:

> It has occurred to me that maybe the whole evaluation movement started off on a couple of false premises which we are now realizing. One is that there is such a thing as a social program, in the sense of a treatment which applied to people which can then be evaluated to see if it works or not. Most of the evaluations we have been talking about, at the government level anyway, assumed that we were providing something to people, that we could say what it was, that we could define some sort of output, and that we could measure whether it took place or not. Well, most of the sorrow of evaluation, it seems to us, stems from that basic lack of realism, as well as the uninterpretable results that the typical study has produced. [46]

On a related front, Donald Schon speaks to the distinction between the high ground of theory and the low ground of practice:

> In the varied topography of professional practice, there is a high ground overlooking a swamp. On the high ground, management problems lend themselves to solutions through the application of research-based theory and technique. In the swamp lowland, messy, confusing problems defy technical solutions...The practitioner must choose. Shall he remain on the high ground where he can solve prevailing standards of rigor, or shall he descend to the swamp of important problems and non-rigorous inquiry? [47]

Evaluations certainly have their place. Some impressive major assessments, such as national studies of the Head Start Program, have proven highly effective in shaping public policy on a large scale. Useful evaluations have two characteristics. First, they are focused on major programs that have become established over time. A program template has emerged that can remain reasonably constant. Second, the evaluation is relatively free-standing. From the investor's perspective, the evaluation is a project. It can have its own performance targets tied to evaluation use outcomes and its own milestones.

Toward Verification

If the investors' needs are not readily satisfied by formal programs of evaluation, what should be done to define return on investment? Our answer begins with a simplification. While funders talk of "measuring results" and determining "levels of outcome," investors see their question more starkly. Did the implementors reach their target? This turns the problem from *measurement* to *verification.*

Implementors have a responsibility to offer evidence at the end of the project on the extent to which they achieved their performance targets. This chore should not be onerous, since they will have been tracking performance very closely as the projects unfolded. Indeed, the verification strategies we will discuss are as applicable during a project as after it.

The verification process begins with a literal tallying. If a project indicated that ten people would get a job or five hundred people would visit a clinic, implementors can count and report the actual number who took those steps. The definition of targets is tangible and often behavioral terms is the key to such basic verification. If quality jobs are defined in a target as specified levels of pay and fringe benefits, job-holder preference, and mobility, these dimensions can be observed as well as the job itself. If the target is "higher self-esteem" or "better communications" however, verification is difficult at best.

Just as verification is distinct from most forms of evaluation, so too is it different from the database and "case management" systems used in human services. These tracking systems provide information on the number and nature of people being served, speed of need response, and timeliness of case close-out. Generally, however, they do not tell us if a customer has changed his or her behavior or achieved another benefit. In general, we suggest that verification be seen as a separate, streamlined task, not as an added component in a complex data system which is as likely to be in development or transition as it is to be fully operational at any given time. Verification cannot wait.

One straightforward approach to verification is to ask customers to talk directly about changes which did or did not happen for them. Implementors can call 20 or 200 persons and ask them if they did what the program intended them to do. While in some cases an independent viewpoint may be needed to control for distortion, this direct approach recognizes that one real expert on what has happened to and/or for a person, or has been caused by a person, is *that* person.

One useful strategy in self-reporting is to compensate people for their help. If 100 persons are each paid $25 when they hold a telephone or personal conversation with a verifier, the total cost is $2,500. The cost of simply tracking down that number of persons and getting together with them (especially for follow-up verifications) will likely far exceed that total. Customer payment, of course, should itself be performance-based.

Personal verification with customers can have a strong effect, especially when announced in advance, in pushing a project toward success. When customers know that what happens to them will be remembered, they are more likely to undertake the desired change in order to be able to report it.

Indeed, smart implementors will often spark customer accountability in an explicit way. As the program opens, an implementor might say:

> The target for this activity, as you know, is to stimulate exercise. You need to know that the people who gave us the money to give you this course—and we ourselves—will not be happy just because you choose to attend all the sessions, or tell us that you found the information valuable. We will only be pleased if at least twenty of you begin and sustain exercise at least three times each week.
>
> You should know that one month and then six months after the program, we will call you to ask if this has happened. If five or more of you are unable to honestly report exercising three times each week, we will have failed. The result focus for this workshop is actually more up to you than us.

The argument might be made that this is an unfair announcement, that it biases people toward outcomes that they would not otherwise achieve. Some may add that what is demonstrated is not workshop efficacy, but the so-called "Hawthorne Effect" of people performing at a higher level when they believe that they are special. Our answer is, "That's great." If implementors could help everyone who has a problem to feel they are part of an experiment in which they personally matter, all the better.

Another strategy opens up with customer contact: to continue the program itself through follow-up verification. An extra half-hour on the phone or in person may make all the difference in getting results, which can then be logged. Picture the person who has sat through five workshop sessions and who has a clear explanation for why he or she has not finished his or her school credits within three months, which was the performance target. Rather than record failure, why not respond by working out a new strategy and then calling the person in a week to see if it has begun to work? This can be very cost-effective. [48] Survey research experience suggests that you can double your returns with one or more follow-up contacts with those who do not respond to the first mailing. If this is true for a peripheral activity, think of its value when applied to customers who are already invested!

While verification determines the extent to which performance targets have been reached, it can also be used to add meaning after, as well as during, a project. When a person does not contribute to reaching a performance target, for example, it is certainly appropriate to ask the reasons. Indeed, explanations from customers are far more valuable than are explanations from implementors.

Some customer questions may well ask for feelings or insights that cannot readily be expressed in a question/response format. In those instances, a useful tool that deepens the personal insight level of project verification is the diary.

Here are a few passages of diaries kept by US residents of Stump Creek Pennsylvania, a small mining town in Appalachian Pennsylvania.[49] Residents were working to renew their town in partnership with The Rensselaerville Institute, and shared their diaries with Institute staff.

> I noticed all the women in the clique were at the schoolhouse to do some cleaning while the other women were ignored as usual. As far as I am concerned, I can do without them and I don't know whether I want to become involved with anything that goes on in the town.

This passage was pivotal in understanding why a performance target on participation was not being met. No adjustments in the program (tasks, rewards, importance, etc.) would matter until the clique problem was addressed.

> I get the feeling that when I talk to some people, they just don't believe that all this is going to happen. And that really disturbs me because if they can't take the chance to better themselves, they just seem to be saying they give up or else quit altogether.

This diary insight helped everyone to see a persistent sense of resignation, even in the midst of evident renewal. The following passage—from another diarist—helped explain the reason:

> Perhaps the difficult times of the Depression left an indelible mark on me. A fear that the affluence of this country might crack as it did before. There are times I think everyone might profit by a short period of no money, no work, getting by with what one has.

As a result of this insight, the project was recast in "bootstrapping" terms, which replaced the original grand dreams and expectations with an "inch at a time" philosophy. It worked.

Note that these examples of citizen expressions remain in the verification rather than measurement mode. They were efforts to define residents' feelings and beliefs which were relevant to project success. Note also that verification in this sense relate to milestones as well as to targets. Insights led to course corrections.

Verification can also be applied to the baseline projection on which a performance target has been set. As discussed earlier, without a forecast of what would most likely happen to people in the absence of program participation, a performance target has little meaning. A comparison group—matched as closely as possible to customers of a given project—can be defined and tracked. Only then does the value of achieving a performance target become known for some programs.

Consider a program which presumed that of the hundred teen-aged women with whom it would work, forty will likely get pregnant in the normal course of events. The target is to go from this projected baseline to no more than fifteen pregnancies per hundred people. If about forty young women in the comparison group do in fact became pregnant, the investment proves effective. If sixty women in the control group become pregnant, the target of fifteen looks even more impressive. But if only sixteen women in the control group became pregnant, the performance target plummets in value. It may well have been achieved with no program at all!

Again, as with the initial formation of a baseline, we stress that approximations are often acceptable, which is why we speak of a "comparison" group rather than of the precise "control" group of evaluation terms. Investors cannot—and need not—afford high precision in many of their projects. They use data as a signpost, a basis for insight, and a "best guess" investment strategy, not to determine an absolute conclusion. Where it is warranted, a separate evaluation project can be defined—and in its own Outcome terms, of course.

The Investor's Role in Verification

To this point we have discussed the implementor's responsibility in verification. We now conclude with a focus on steps the investor might take.

In business, investors look carefully at monthly or financial reports prepared by management. At the end of each year, they seek a financial audit done by an independent firm. This is both a check on accuracy of those keeping score for an enterprise and a way of guarding against deliberate misrepresentation. Audits generally proceed in two steps. First, they understand and verify the kinds of procedures used—for cash control, allocation of expenses, and other matters. Second, they provide spot checks and tests to ensure that accepted accounting principles are followed and that the calculations are accurate. They might, for example, pick at random the expense reports of three of twenty employees to check for adequate documentation of reimbursement claims.

In government programs, a similar kind of investor scrutiny is possible. Either through their own staff or an independent agent, we strongly recommend an auditing function. If unaffordable as routine practice, random audits of projects supported are sufficient as long as everyone believes that there is a reasonable chance that their number can come up.

In many cases, verification checks will not prove costly. If a program warrants that 28 of its customers have experienced a desired change, the project auditor might examine the log sheet of customer verifications, then call four of these individuals directly. If a project has served a thousand people, it is still not impossible to sample customers in a cost-effective way. In many instances, the investment agent defined in Chapter 8 can perform the auditing function. He or she is already familiar with the performance targets and milestones of their groups financed.

With results verified, scrutiny in most grant-making tends to focus on low-performing projects. In Outcome Funding, an unexpected success can be more valuable than an unanticipated failure. After validating the results from a high-performing group, the investor may choose to place more pounds with that group. It is generally far more cost-effective to add to high performance than to spend money to remediate low performance. [50]

Chapter 15

Learning

Experience, it is said, is a great teacher. If this is true, we must conclude that most of us who have experiences tend to be poor students. Most projects or products financed by government look remarkably similar in their second year to their configuration in the first year. Investors also tend to send out the same proposal formats, use the same criteria, and even select the same groups year after year. The problem is not that implementor and investor have not evaluated or even verified. It is that they have not learned.

Learning is a key term in Outcome Funding, and this chapter is devoted to its meaning, applications, and formats. We begin with definition.

Educators and psychologists generally agree on the definition of learning as "a relatively enduring change in behavior." [51] Learning means that people change their practices to improve over time. In a learning organization, very little stays the same. In the private sector, the learning curve of an organization is so important that a person who has tried something, failed, and learned from the mistake is often favored over one who has never erred. The latter may have all his or her mistakes left to make!

Learning requires two forms of openness. One is openness to information from the project's environment, especially from its customers. Without fresh input from project experience, there is no reason to revisit initial assumptions. The second is openness to error and mistake. Without a sense that current activities are either misguided or at least falling short of potential, why change? Error is so critical that Donald Michaels deems it a key for accountability in the learning organization:

> An essential aspect of accountability would be the requirement that a person or organization demonstrate that appropriate actions were taken to seek out errors and openly report them. Under this norm, what would be punished would be the *failure* to embrace error. Technical competence would be partially measured by the ability to detect error, and the ability to use information gained for learning more about where to head and how to get there. [52]

Much is known about learning as a discipline and practice, and at least some of its principles have been agreed upon. An example is the notion that behavior which is rewarded from the learner's point of view is more likely to recur than behavior which is not. Different learning theories agree that repetition without reward is a poor way to learn—that is, to change.

Adults as Learners

Before turning to learning applications in Outcome Funding, let's look at those students in organizations that invest and implement in projects for public benefit.

While learning is often equated with education in a formal sense, a great deal of it happens well beyond the age of school children and well beyond the bounds of classrooms. As philosopher Mortimer Adler observes:

> I can hardly remember...when I had the mistaken notion that the schools were the most important part of the educational process; for now I think exactly the reverse. I am now convinced that it is adult education which is the substantial and major part

> of the educational process—the part for which all the rest is at best—and it is at its best only when it is—a preparation. [53]

Such sentiments are supported by practice as well as ideals. Allen Tough's extensive study of adult learning projects (which he defines as major, highly-deliberative efforts to gain certain knowledge and skill) suggests that the typical adult spends about seven hundred hours per year in some eight learning projects. [54] Tough further concludes that most adults are not motivated by credit in such forms as degrees or certifications and that only about ten percent of learning projects are associated with educational institutions. Among Tough's most important conclusions for our purposes is that adults do not necessarily need formal teaching. While they almost always turn to someone for help in the learning sequence, they seldom turn to professional educators.

Adult learning approaches in organizations can take many forms. A useful example is called "action learning." It involves small teams of people who identify problems and develop a research design to gather and interpret relevant data to their problem. It is an alternative to most modes of training in that the material is not books or written case studies, but dynamic problems and opportunities of the organization itself. Action learning for businesses and other organizations provides a means for learning to develop "questioning insight" from experience rather than rely on expert-programmed knowledge.

One key to the successful engagement of managers in action learning is empowerment. The learner controls the process. And the learner has the most to gain, as Foy notes in a *Harvard Business Review* article:

> Action learning seems to be the one so-called

> “technique” that encourages this entire spectrum of skills necessary for management today. With careful planning, an action learning program can result in high marks for fact- finding, diagnosis, creativity, decision-making, and learning how to communicate with and motivate people to take action themselves. [55]

In stressing adults as students, one virtue of childhood inquiry remains critical to effective Outcome Funding. Peter Senge observes that the impulse in children to learn goes beyond coping with environmental change, to an impulse to generate new possibilities. He concludes that “This is why leading corporations are focusing on *generative* learning, which is about creating, as well as *adaptive* learning, which is about coping.”[56]

Lessons Learned

How many times do we hear people say how much they have learned from an experience? Yet if people are challenged to name three specific insights gained from a conference, project, book or whatever they will use to change their behavior in a specified way, many are silent. The equivalent of a math or an English lesson in school is a lesson from experience. Whatever the label, learning is generally enabled by explicit and focused findings, which often serve as a pin prick to prompt action. Here’s an example:

> The Rensselaerville Institute mounted a comprehensive physical and social renewal program in the small village of Stump Creek, Pennsylvania. Based on journals kept by project staff, one of the many lessons that emerged from the project was this one:
>
> DON’T: underestimate the power of symbolism. In Stump Creek, almost every time we (staff and residents) tried a symbolic omen, it worked—and

usually in proportion to our belief in it. Community celebrations, inaugurations (i.e., of the library or the water tank) went well. Conversely, events which did *not* have a symbolic value did not tend to sustain. In part, we did not find the limits of symbolism.

DO: press more boldly to explore the value of images and symbols. More unusual events—whether sunrise prayer services or all-night vigils or creation of special places or times of day or holidays in community—may work well. Nothing learned in Stump Creek would suggest that even a community covenant would not work. [57]

The Institute subsequently mounted a similar project with the village of Corbett, a declined hamlet in Appalachian New York. The above lesson led directly to the idea of an agreement by which to express the values and symbols important to village residents. The Corbett Compact was developed by residents and publicly signed. The document proved to have a profound effect on enabling the renewal project, and is now studied nationally as a model of citizen cooperation. Here is its Preamble, a direct outcome of the learning methodology.

THE CORBETT COMPACT

We, the members of the Village of Corbett and The Institute of Man and Science [renamed The Rensselaerville Institute], set forth on an adventure which requires our full cooperation and commitment. Like the passengers on the ship Mayflower, we draft and sign this compact setting forth some articles of common faith and agreement.

In doing so, we give our pledge to rebuild Corbett as

a small community in which people help each other... in which we can get a good night's sleep...in which our children can range safely...in which we can feel good about our town, our neighbors, and ourselves... in which we do not waste.

At the same time, we seek a community in which people live and let live, respecting the rights of others to be different. We want people to grow. Some will grow and stay. Others will grow and leave. But for all of us, Corbett may always be home. [58]

One useful device is the "Lessons Learned Forum." Investors can convene groups with projects in the same area to share their own project experiences. In this sense, the investor becomes a repository and broker of learnings. This imagery might even suggest a Learning Bank. This bank would be similar in function to a financial institution, in that it welcomes both deposits and withdrawals. On one hand, each learner for a given project could be charged with making at least one "deposit" in the sense of a project learning deemed relevant to other staff members in the organization. On the other, each learner could also be asked to make a "withdrawal" by indicating at least one learning from another person which he or she wished to apply or test in his or her own learning. A section of the learning plan could be added to express the banking activity of those involved.

This slightly whimsical format may also help free people from current practice and attitudes toward evaluation and documentation. At the same time, the banking analogy is useful for organizational growth. A better resource than learning is hard to imagine.

Investors need "lessons learned" as much as do project implementors. Among the questions their learnings can address:

- Where we made a bad bet, what led us astray and what should we do differently next time?

- In what ways did our grant application requests confuse applicants or make it difficult for them to frame effective projects?

- What did we learn from investor agents about how better to support projects in which we invest?

- What did we learn about milestone and milestone management that should be shared with project implementors?

- Did we interest new organizations? What do we now know about those who saw our grant application requests and chose not to apply?

The Learning Plan

The Learning Plan is a vocational equivalent of the learning contract, a device whose value is well-documented in formal education and continuing adult education. Malcolm Knowles, an adult education specialist, nicely summarizes the strengths of this approach:

> Without question, the single most potent tool I have come across in my forty-three years of experience with adult education is contract learning. It has solved more problems that plagued me during my first forty years than any other invention. It solves the problem of the wide range of backgrounds, education, experience, interests, motivations, and abilities that characterize most adult groups by providing a way for individuals (and sub-groups) to tailor-make their own learning plans. It solves the problem of

getting the learner to have a sense of ownership of the objectives he or she will pursue. It solves the problem of identifying a wide variety of resources so that different learners can go to different resources for learning the same things. It solves the problem of providing each learner with a visible structure for systemizing his or her learning. Finally, it solves the problem of providing a systematic procedure for involving the learner's responsibility in evaluating the learning outcomes. [59]

Learning Plans are literal documents that begin by specifying the name and stake of all learners, and can include customers, investors, and critics as well as project leaders and staff. The driving force is at least one learning question which has these characteristics: [60]

- It is specific, not general, and is connected in a clear way to milestones or targets;

- It is possible to bring information of some sort to bear on the question and to attempt reasonable response. Further, it is possible to specify the kinds of sources of information relevant to the question;

- There is more than one possible answer, and the learner has not already made up his or her mind about which answer is correct; and

- The learner is asking the question for him- or herself, not as a surrogate for others.

Learning plans also require specificity as to how the individual asking the question will use the information. One critical element of use is decision-making. If the inquirer cannot think of one decision he or she must make that can be guided by the answer to a critical question, why bother to ask it? Another aspect is personal change. In many surveys and questionnaires, while everyone may agree that a question is important, no one is prepared to say what influence the answer will have on one's own behavior. The learning plan is an excellent choice for getting to essentials.

Just as projects are more often based on individual energies and capacities than on collective resources, so too is learning. As one education theorist puts it:

> Organizations do not consume information; people do—individual, idiosyncratic, caring, uncertain, searching people who are in a position to make all the difference in the world from the perspective of utilization of information. To ignore the personal factor is to diminish utilization potential from the outset. To target evaluations at organizations is to target them at nobody in particular—and, in effect, not to really target the evaluation at all. [61]

Additional elements of the learning plan focus on the verification or research strategy to be used, the data needed to answer the question, and any interpretive framework that may be needed.

32. In employment, for example, an entry-level job at or near minimum wage is not likely to be sustained. The job holder will at some point realize that the net income from not working is higher than that from working! In this instance, the qualitative dimensions of the pay level, fringe benefits, and enjoyment must enter if this result is to be sustained.

33. From an outcome perspective, "equal access"—whether by persons who are poor, minority, or disenfranchised—is often not enough precisely because it is an input. What matters is the result from access. If some persons tend to benefit greatly from programs and others seem generally not to be helped, questions of product selectivity are usefully raised.

34. Florida performance targets cited in Jack A. Brizius and Michael D. Campbell, *Getting Results*. Washington: Council of Governors' Policy Advisors, 1991, pp. 8-9. The book has numerous other examples, as well as a performance accountability system format at the policy level.

35. For a look at this misguided approach to costing a meeting see: Harold S. Williams, "Rx: Save Your Meeting," *Corporate Meetings and Incentives*, November, 1987.

36. Our stale imagery traps us. The notion of a net connotes catching and retaining fish, tigers and perhaps human creatures who must then passively await help or harm. From an outcome perspective, let's think of a safety trampoline, from which people can bounce back up!

37. Cited in "Workers: Risks and Rewards," *TIME Magazine*, April 15, 1991.

38. For insight on this phenomenon in education see Robert Rosenthal and Lenore Jacobon, *Pygmalion in the Classroom.* New York: Irvington, 1989.

39. David McClelland's research and findings are summarized in his book, *The Achieving Society.* Princeton: Van Nostrand, 1961.

40. For a summary of research in this area, see, "An Assessment of Substance Abuse Prevention," a working paper of the Office of Prevention, New York State Division of Substance Abuse Services, October, 1989.

41. The idea of goals displacement as organizational distortion was first explored some 60 years ago by the German sociologist Robert Michaels. It occurs not in so much in leadership as in the very body of the organization. Consider this passage by Philip Selznick:

    > Running an organization, as a specialized and essential activity, generates problems which have no necessary (and often opposed) relationship to the professed or "original" goals of the organization. The day-to-day behavior of the group becomes centered around specific problems and approximate goals which have primarily an internal relevance. Then, since these activities come to consume an increasing proportion of the time and thoughts of the participants, they are—from the point of view of actual behavior—substitutes for the professed goals. (Cited in: Sills, David, *The*

Volunteers. Glencoe, The Free Press, 1957.)

In many ways, the current grant-making process, focussed as it is on inputs, itself reflects a goals displacement.

42. While we think of non-profit and other groups responding to public purposes as having high aspirations, many do not. Instead of hitching their wagons to stars, many hitch their stars to wagons—called activity.

43. Pre-qualifying customers is a key to effective private sector selling. Building companies, for example, are fond of two initial questions: "Do you have a site on which the home can be built?" and "Will you need our help in financing the home?" Those customers with land are ten times more likely to proceed that those without, and those who do not need help in getting a mortgage are much more likely to have a good credit rating than those who do. For non-profit and government agency examples, see Harold S. Williams, *Marketing Government Programs*. New York: The Rensselaerville Institute, 1991.

44. Adrian Fasset, Project Director of Employment Opportunities Council of Suffolk (New York), a group using Outcome Funding under a State grant from the New York State Department of Social Services. Contained in "On the Results and Milestone Approach," an Innovation Case Study, of The Innovation Group, Rensselaerville, New York, p. 3.

45. This quote is from the document noted in footnote 44.

46. Passage is by Alice Rivlin of The Brookings Institute, from a panel discussion included in Clark Abt, ed, *The Evaluation of Social Programs*. Beverly Hills: Sage Press, 1976, p. 237.

47. Schon, Donald, *Educating the Reflective Practitioner*. San Francisco: Jossey-Bass, 1987, p. 3.

48. For example, if a group has a grant of $40,000 to do something for 80 people and if results are achieved for 40 of these persons, the cost for each person helped is $1,000. An average of two hours of added staff time at $20. per hour to boost as well as verify results for each customer would add a total of $3,200. If four people move toward a result that would otherwise not get there, the verification has more than paid for itself.

49. The diary citations are from: Williams, Harold S., Swanson, Bert E., and Linton, Kenneth, *The Restoration of Stump Creek: Volume II, A Community Profile*. New York: The Rensselaerville Institute, 1980.

50. In many cases, additional monies granted to high performing groups is the best of all possible investments. Not only has the group demonstrated high competence but it may well be able to add customers and results at a lower cost than that required for the initial customers it served. The marginal or added costs to serve still one more person when the fixed expenses (e.g., materials, staff, etc.) have already been covered can be low.

51. As an example of typical learning definitions:

Learning involves change. It is concerned with the acquisition of habits, knowledge, and attitudes. It enables the learner to make both personal and social adjustments. (Burton, H.H., "Basic Principles in a Good Teaching-Learning Situation," in Crow, ed., *Readings in Human Learning*. New York: McKay, 1963.)

52. Donald, M. Michael, *On Learning to Plan and Planning to Learn*. San Francisco: Jossey-Bass, 1976, p. 141.

53. Adler's comment appears in his essay, "Why Only Adults Can Be Educated" in *A Guidebook to Learning*. New York: McMillan, 1986.

54. Tough, Allen, *The Adults' Learning Projects: A Fresh Approach to Theory and Practice in Adult Learning*. Toronto: The Ontario Institute for Studies in Education, 1979.

55. Foy, Nancy, "Action Learning Comes to Industry," *Harvard Business Review*, September/October, 1977, pp. 158-159.

56. Senge, Peter M. , "The Leaders New Work: Building Learning Organizations," *Sloan Management Review*, Fall, 1990.

57. Schautz, Jane, and Pholar, Stephen C., *Lessons Learned From Stump Creek*. Rensselaerville, NY: The Rensselaerville Institute, 1980.

58. For the complete Corbett Compact and its meaning for a community change project see Hawley, Natalie and Williams, Harold S., "The Corbett Compact," in *Small Town*, Vol 10, Nos. 7-8, 1980.

59. Knox, Alan B., *Adult Development and Learning.* San Francisco: Jossey-Bass, 1977.

60. We are grateful to Michael Q. Patton for his keen insight on questions for assessment as described in his book, *Utilization-Focused Evaluation.* Beverly Hills: Sage Press, 1978.

61. Patton, 1978.

PART IV:

The Special Case of Innovation

Develop only the bare minimum to prove an idea, prove only one idea at a time, never develop what can be bought or modified, minimize the time to demonstration, insist on the highest standards of workmanship, and do all of this with the smallest possible team.

J.A. Kuechen

Chapter 16

The Entrepreneur as Mover and Shaker

We have noted at several points that implementors can be as important as the program design in achieving results. In the case of innovation projects, the human factor is essential. Innovations do not tend to come from plans or from committees; they most often come from a people. Behind the innovation is the innovator. Indeed, investors who wish to forecast the likelihood that an innovation will work are advised to look carefully at the innovator. This is our starting point in Part IV. We begin with a look at one group of innovators known by another name. Their story illuminates the drive and focused energy innovators need to overcome obstacles and the inertia of tradition.

Innovation and the Entrepreneurial Act

American Fred Smith had an idea. He wanted to fly everyone's package to one central point in Tennessee late at night and then distribute letters and parcels to their destinations before lunch the next day. When Fred shared his idea with others, including a professor at Yale, they were not encouraging. At that point, packages were all shipped like mail—directly from one point to another. It took Fred several venture capital firm presentations but he finally found a backer. One of the most successful enterprises in America, Federal Express, was born.

Whether glamorous or mundane, the businesses in which venture capitalists invest tend to share one characteristic: they are based on an innovation. No matter how effectively run, most businesses share the market with similar enterprises and tend to conform to the profit curves established for that industry. For high return, however, something new is needed. Peter Drucker puts the connection clearly:

> Innovation is the specific instrument of entrepreneurship. It is the act that endows resources with a new capacity to create wealth. Innovation, indeed, creates a resource. There is no such thing as a "resource" until man finds a use for something in nature and thus endows it with economic value. Until then, every plant is a weed and every mineral just another rock. [62]

There is also a historical relationship between entrepreneurs and innovation. The foremost early theorist on the concept was Joseph Schumpeter, who in the early 1900s developed his concept of the entrepreneur not as risk-taker, but as *innovator*, distinguishing himself or herself by carrying out "new combinations" of enterprise formation. The entrepreneur to Schumpeter "is a special kind of person, creative in bringing about growth through the process of making changes...It is the special process of change that sets the entrepreneur apart from all others." [63] To Schumpeter, entrepreneurship as innovation is an act of *will*, not of *intellect*. He defines entrepreneurs not as who they are, but as what they do.

Some observers see broad patterns of entrepreneurially-driven change. James Brian Quinn has said:

> Historically, Western societies have depended on the individual inventor/entrepreneur for many of their most startling innovations. In fact, this "individual entrepreneurial system" has proved history's most successful method for meeting new human needs.[64]

Even changes presumed caused by other factors may have been sparked, upon closer look, by an entrepreneurial act. For example, in the US, the famous Hawthorne Studies at Western Electric, conducted in the 1930s, led to the discovery of the now-legendary "Hawthorne Effect." Briefly put, it means that when social supports (such as the atmosphere of an experiment and attendant management attention) are provided, productivity will rise. Thousands of undergraduate pupils were taught this effect as a basic principle of organization. Recent studies which re-examined the database of the Hawthorne studies, however, have unearthed a different finding—one virtually ignored in the original studies. Although not part of the experiment, a change in workers took place during the Hawthorne experiments. As one study has found, "It was with the introduction of the highly-motivated operator with leadership qualities that output began its steady impressive climb."[65] In reality, the Hawthorne study may show that when a specific individual with "unusual character and motivation" is introduced into a small team, substantive improvement begins.

Characteristics of Entrepreneurs

One group of investors has made something of a science of selecting innovators. Venture capital firms find and bet on entrepreneurs. But unlike banks and most other institutional investors, they are not looking for an assured rate of return on their money. Rather, they become part owners of new or expanding businesses which appear to have the promise of fame and fortune. For those enterprises that do take off, the venture capital firm may get ten or more dollars back for every one invested. At the same time, for those that fail, the investment must often be written off entirely.

Venture capitalists are presented annually with hundreds of would-be entrepreneurs, each fervently believing that his or her idea will make millions of dollars in short order. These investors have developed a substantial body of research to help them define and select entrepreneurs on the basis of traits or characteristics.

Most studies are empirical rather than theoretical. They begin by putting successful entrepreneurs in one pile and other individuals in another and asking, "What's the difference?"

Among the twenty attributes usually generated by studies of entrepreneurs, here are six distinguishing characteristics that show up most repeatedly in the literature.

- *High degree of personal responsibility.* Entrepreneurs don't tend to blame God, fate, or luck for what happens to them. Rather, they feel that they are responsible for outcomes. (Psychologists label this as a high "internal locus of control.") This is generally seen as related to a high need for achievement. [66]

- *Excellent use of feedback.* Entrepreneurs in a business context have often failed at least once before they succeed. But they can relate exactly why and how they failed, and are clear that they would not make the same mistakes again.

- *Divergent in thinking.* One of the greatest sparks for an entrepreneur is the expression "It can't be done." Entrepreneurs tend to circumvent traditional thinking to find new routes to old destinations. They tend not to see problems but rather opportunities.

- *Moderately high risk-taking.* Entrepreneurs are willing and able to invest their own money and their reputation in solving a problem by creating a new solution. At the same time, they wish to ensure that the factors leading to success are under their control. [67]

- *Tenacity*. Entrepreneurs are generally characterized by a steadfast determination which is narrowly and intensely expressed. Entrepreneurs are not out to save the world, but to achieve an important performance target.

- *Optimistic and enthusiastic nature*. Most entrepreneurs are optimistic—often overly so—about what their innovations can do. It is an optimism born not in a general rosy faith (everything turns out for the best), but in a conviction that they can pull off their dreams. With optimism comes great energy, and often zeal.

Studies on these and other factors are not unequivocal, and care must be taken in using them in a selection process. Characteristics associated with successful entrepreneurs become guides but not, in themselves, a full predictor. Also, note the great number of dimensions in which no particular trait is named. Entrepreneurs may be old or young, short or tall, male or female. They may be extroverts or introverts, highly educated or not formally educated.

Other scholars stress the cultural and social factors, which influence entrepreneurial behavior (rather than psychological ones). Albert Shapero is among those who offer strong evidence that entrepreneurs are often conceived in an act of *displacement*. His studies show that many people become entrepreneurs when they are fired or otherwise dislodged from a comfortable state of being. Generally, far more entrepreneurs seem to have been forged more from adverse pushes (such as being fired) than from positive pulls (such as an inheritance to provide capital).

Shapero integrates psychological, social, and economic

factors with a company-formation process model involving four elements needed by the nascent entrepreneur: [68]

- Displacement—a situational variable;
- A disposition to act—a psychological propensity;
- Examples of behavior that impart credibility—a social factor; and
- Availability of adequate resources for starting a new venture—an economic variable.

While assuming different mixes of psychological, social, and cultural factors, most contemporary scholars of entrepreneurship agree that entrepreneurs are produced in a society by non-economic reasons. They are then seen as available to intervene in the economic arena—and in other arenas as well.

While academics carry the definitional quest to a lawful end, venture capitalists want to know only enough to place the best possible bets. They have no interest in the paper specifications of an ideal entrepreneur—unless one can be built to those exact dimensions. When all is said and done, they define entrepreneurs by only one measure: their results.

Entrepreneurs by Comparison

Entrepreneurs can also be understood in comparison to other functions. The most classic comparison in business is between entrepreneurs who are needed to start businesses and managers who are needed to run them once they are established. Entrepreneurs continually want to improve products, even when they are perfectly acceptable to everyone else. And entrepreneurs operate at a level of intensity that others cannot and will not match. Histories of failed enterprises are rife with pioneers who stayed too long at the party they created. Managers, in contrast, bring needed codification and routine to enterprises once they are formed. While indispensable to smooth and predictable operation, managers are much less likely to provide the adaptive ability to handle new conditions.

Equally important is the distinction between the inventor who conceives of a new product and the entrepreneur who makes something of it. The risk to the inventor is that it won't work. The risk to the entrepreneur is that it cannot be shaped or priced in a way that is acceptable to customers. The trade-off between these functions is not always smooth, Shapero notes:

> More often than not, an invention finds its way into public use through the actions of an entrepreneur who must pry it loose from the grasp of its creator before it realizes its potential in the marketplace. [69]

The distinction for innovation holds up well. "Creative people" in organizations are honored for having bright ideas. In reality, ideas—no matter how brilliant—are plentiful. What is rare is an individual who can take an idea—regardless of source —and do something with it. Innovators apply ideas, and in many cases, could care less where they originated.

Consider the case of Bette Nesbith Graham, a secretary in a Texas Bank when IBM introduced the carbon ribbon typewriter.[70] With this machine, the conventional practice of erasing errors led only to smudges. In her work with artists who painted holiday scenes on the bank's plate windows, Bette observed a similar problem. She noticed that when artists painted green where red should go, they did not try to erase the wrong color. Instead, they painted white paint over the color, then applied the correct one.

Bette borrowed some of the paint and began to use it at her typewriter to correct typing errors. The application that led her to found "liquid paper" (which she later sold to Gillette for many millions of dollars) was born. Bette was not the "inventor" of this idea. Indeed, she simply moved it twenty feet and put it to work in a new way. This is the point of many, if not most, innovations.

Two additional distinctions emerge as we focus on innovators who use government funds for public purposes. The first is between planners and doers. Some people have a predisposition to study, to research, to prepare. They believe that implementation should occur only when a plan is complete. Innovators have a predisposition to act. They are impatient to try something.

A second distinction is between innovators and advocates. Both have energy, commitments, and a results focus. The difference is that advocates are primarily concerned with defending rights, and innovators are concerned with meeting needs. These goals may be compatible, but they are not equivalent.

Entrepreneurs Beyond Business

While the entrepreneur is traditionally defined in the context of business, this does not appear to be a generic limitation. Entrepreneurs seek out private enterprise because it can most readily satisfy their needs, including:

- Freedom to create *new ventures* (i.e., ease of new business formation);

- A way to clearly *measure* success and failure (i.e., through profits and growth);

- Immediate *feedback* on performance (i.e., sales level or customer comments);

- A chance to be personally *responsible* (i.e., the factor seen as critical in success or failure); and

- Ability to be *rewarded* for performance (i.e., remuneration on an incentive basis).

Entrepreneurship is set apart from other modes of purposeful activity less on the basis of its targets on the path used to get there. The evidence is strong, for example, that money to the innovator is a way not of getting rich but of keeping score. Indeed, studies of those who leave corporations to create new ventures generally find that the primary reason is not dissatisfaction with pay or benefits, but rather their lack of freedom to innovate.

When these conditions can be met, entrepreneurs can be found in diverse settings, including the kinds of non-profit and community-based groups funded by government. Interviews in Bill Berkowitz' fascinating book called *Local Heroes* make this point eloquently. In terms of a disposition to act, listen to these American community-based sparkplugs: [71]

- I couldn't get anybody else. Actually, I tried at least a dozen different friends of mine to do it. They never were interested. "I'm too busy with something else." "I want to be with my grandchildren." "I want to take a trip to Europe." They weren't interested. People that I considered my bosom friends—not interested. And I said, well, if there's nobody else that will do it, I'll have to do it myself. (Homer Fahrner, founder of Senior Gleaners—a group that picks up and redistributes surplus food.)

- So I was in that slump of just arriving home, and I went for the phone, picked it up, and started calling local convalescent homes and said, "I'm a performer, and I'm interested to know if you'd like to have some music brought for no cost...." (Mimi Farina, founder of Bread and Roses, a group that brings professional entertainment to people in institutions.)

And in considering the trait of energy, enthusiasm and optimism, these observations reflect its diverse sources: [72]

- I will hook people. I'll talk them into it. I'll con them into doing something that they don't really...'cause I can beat them down with sheer enthusiasm. Back in the privacy of their room, they're not sure they want to do it at all. And I've overdone it a couple of times, on that basis. You know what I mean, I've carried them along or swept them along with my enthusiasm or excitement about doing something. (Marti Stevens, founder of Cornwallville, Maine, Players.)

- The sense of outrage I have is tremendous. You know, when you read in the paper, like there's another program that's cut—it really makes you mad, angry. Not because it's another issue, but because you can see, you can picture, you can picture what it means. You can practically picture the faces of the people, or you can see the person sleeping on a grate. These are people. And these people have children. That's what keeps you motivated; that's what keeps you going. (Fran Froehlich, founder, Poor People's United Fund.)

Entrepreneurial Strategies

Entrepreneurs tend to use a handful of strategies that have

high relevance for innovators. Here are four.

Utilization of resources.

Most people, whether in corporations or government, have an acquisitive approach to resources. Whether people, money, equipment, or supplies, their desire is to own and control. This is natural since more organizations mistakenly reward people for having larger budgets and more people "under" them. The acquisitive approach also leads to a consolidation and solidification of resources. The owner and controller do not wish to risk giving up what they have taken great pains to collect. Indeed, they find more reinforcement in having resources than in using them. In the acquisitive mode, resources are additive. Five people are five more people.

Entrepreneurs, in contrast, are much more interested in using resources than in owning them. They are prone to "beg, borrow, or steal" what they need and are even willing to return the resource when they no longer need it. They are far less interested in the amount than in the timing of resources. A thousand dollars or two persons today are worth five thousand dollars or ten persons in a year. Rather than to consolidate resources, they are likely to disperse them—with deployment catalyzing action. Finally, they seek to combine resources so that through synergy and interaction, one person and one person are the productive equivalent of three persons, if not five.

The control issue concerning resources may also be seen in a broader context. As Rosabeth Moss Kanter reminds us:

> Entrepreneurs—and entrepreneurial organizations—always operate at the edge of their competence, focusing more of their resources and attention on what they do not yet know...than on controlling

what they already know. [73]

This reflection applies equally to the organizatons who could support human sparkplugs.

The opportunity focus.

Most people, whether in business or government, see problems. As a preoccupation, problems actually tend to have many virtues. One is that they are durable and timely. If we leave for a week or even a year, we can fit right in upon return, because the problems have not changed. Problems are also comfortable because they are seen by everyone. Like the weather, we all share in the experience and have a common language with which to discuss it. Further, we need not be initiators: first the problem, then the response. Ironically, the problem orientation is so pervasive that it continues unchecked in some presumably progressive organizational movements, such as the quest for quality. Quality is typically defined as the state of being error-free. If only we could only catch and eliminate problems, perfection would be at hand.

Whether they are cause or consequence of their optimism, most entrepreneurs are not preoccupied with problems. Indeed, many simply don't see them. Their eyes are on opportunities—things that can be done despite problems—or even because of them. If there is a budget cutback, it's the opportunity to eliminate some functions that never worked anyway. If there are strong customer complaints, it's an opportunity to redesign the product.

In sharp contrast to problems, opportunities are time-bound and fragile. They are seen by very few people—often only by the entrepreneur. The opportunity focus is more than a useful way to define projects. It is a way to take initiative. Opportunities are proactive and promote independence.

Leadership by energy.

Entrepreneurs may start alone, but most soon realize that they need help. Although they tend to be poor at many structural and even interpersonal forms of management, many have discovered an alternative which leads with personal conviction. This strategy is increasingly seen as a strong suit in leaders, if not managers. Bennis and Nanus wrote in their book on leadership:

> Management of attention through *vision* is the *creating of focus*. All ninety people interviewed had an agenda, an unparalleled concern with outcome. Leaders are the most results-oriented individuals in the world, and results get attention. Their visions or intentions are compelling and pull people toward them. Intensity coupled with commitment is magnetic. And these intense personalities do not have to coerce people to pay attention; they are so intent on what they are doing that, like a child completely absorbed with creating a sand castle in a sandbox, they draw others in. [74]

Collaborative relationships.

Contrary to popular conception, many people who start something new do not do so as individuals; neither do they use committees or even teams. Rather, they collaborate intensively with one or more other individuals. Famous duos are legendary—Rogers and Hart in theatre, Watson and Crick in science, Hewlett and Packard in business. As Michael Schrage puts it in his book, *Shared Minds*:

> ...collaboration is the process of shared creation: two or more individuals with complementary skills interacting to create a shared understanding that none had previously possessed or could have come to on

> their own. Collaboration creates a shared meaning about a process, a product, or an event. [75]

In contrast, most managers actually encourage separable people and thoughts, which are then brought together through a number of terms—cooperation, coordination, communication. From an entrepreneur's perspective, collaboration eliminates the need for these connectors while enhancing the directness and individuality of achievement.

Entrepreneurs in Perspective

So we don't see entrepreneurs as the sole keys to a kingdom, some perspectives are important to maintain. The first is that entrepreneurs are not the most dutiful and well-mannered people. Their incessant optimism and urge to swim upstream can make them difficult and very hard to like. In social as well as business relationships, they can be abrasive.

The second needed backdrop is the tendency for entrepreneurs to believe their own press. As William Gartner puts it:

> The self-made man has a vested interest in being unique, in believing that the organization maker is born and not made. As a result, when he tells the story of success, he always begins with his childhood. (This is an almost foolproof way to tell you've got a self-made man on your hands, the way certain bright plumage marks a species of bird.) When the self-made man offers advice to budding organization makers, the advice is always to "be like me" or variations on that theme. [76]

In the 1980s media, adulation was readily at hand. As a *Wall Street Journal* article noted,

> For those who missed the equation as it played out in the business press, there was the spate of self-proclaimed heroism that trumped through bookstores throughout the 1980s. If leadership was the new art of management, these autobiographies and pseudo-biographies were portraits of how the new heroes of business practiced their high art. The message was simple and inescapable: The CEO embodied the corporation—values, character, habits, tastes, and all. The CEO was the company. [77]

Reversal attends most excess, and the adulation of entrepreneurs was no exception. In the early 1990s, corporate down-turns and failures from companies driven by high profile chief executives have become plentiful.

Two "morals" come from this perspective. The first is that the entrepreneur's capacity to do harm is as high as his or her capacity to do good. The second is that the entrepreneurial act can and must be spread among many individuals in an enterprise, based on timing, skill, personal convictions, and other factors.

Chapter 17

Buying Programs, Buying Change

Many funders proudly proclaim that they are in business to fund innovative programs. Upon close inspection, the proposals they support do indeed contain the word "innovative"—often on every page. Also included is language suggesting that the project is a model, demonstration, or pilot which will most assuredly be sought for worldwide replication. Sadly, this is where innovation traditionally ends—in rhetoric. The wrapper is new but the substance is not.

Innovation in public service projects has a limited repertoire. In most projects, it has one of three meanings:

- More or less of a conventional ingredient. (This project is innovative given its high level of community involvement or low level of bureaucracy.)

- Combination of elements not normally found together. (This project is innovative in combining three funding streams or including both a businessperson and a humanist.)

- Newer technology. (This project has a computer data base or will include videotaped outreach.)

When innovation is included in a program, it is typically handled as a program element. The innovation component goes into the proposal and the project as do other components. We thus have the "community piece," the "evaluation piece," and the "innovation piece." The problem starts here. Innovation is a core premise, not an add-on.

The discrepancy between innovation funding by word and innovation funding by deed is tragic. Drugs, literacy, crime, homelessness, unaffordable housing and many other problems have proven themselves virtually immune to threadbare solutions. Even with those programs that once worked well, both implementors and customers will eventually lose interest. Picture a business trying to sell products it fashioned in 1970, let alone 1940. It would be bankrupt in days. Yet in the public sector, we are disposed to build still more industrial park sites on Indian reservations, commission still more master plans to promote public housing, and begin yet more funding initiatives where we will spend endless hours on writing and grading proposal papers prior to the act of grant-making.

Definitions and Meanings

When funders consider the meaning of innovation, they do so in order to label certain proposals as innovative and others as not. Often this preoccupation is about newness. Is this program really original? Should it count as new if it was done somewhere else but not here? Is it sufficiently different or distinctive to warrant our support?

The newness focus is misguided. It leads respondents to believe that novelty is the major criterion for funding, and to seek distinctiveness. The problem is that novelty is not the investor's goal. Innovation drives a service or other product to be not different but better. Indeed, a definition of innovation as new sizzle may well rule out some of the investor's very best prospects, while leading to cycles of fads and fancies. As Peter Drucker says, "All effective innovations are breathtakingly simple. Indeed, the greatest praise an innovation can receive is for people to say: "This is obvious. Why didn't I think of it?" [78]

We have advised out grantmaking clients to consider this definition: a project, to qualify for our support, must be stated as an explicit test of a new approach to outperform an existing practice. It is amazing how many "innovative" proposals go away with just this simple definer!

The overall point to remember is that innovation's meaning lies not in what it is but in what it does. Indeed, one useful meaning of innovation for the investor might be called definition by result. If the project does not believe that it will significantly outperform present practice, why bother with it, regardless of how different it might be? And if a project does commit to a remarkably high level of achievement, why worry about a formal qualification for being "innovative"?

Other factors are factors are helpful in signaling the likely presence of an innovation:

- *An individual.* Most innovations are sparked by an individual who feels strongly or even passionately that something old does not work and that something new will work much better. Ideas do not tend to have the same level of energy as do the people who hold them. A proclaimed innovation without an innovator is suspect.

- *An opportunity focus.* Most innovations are focused less on timeless and enduring problems than on time-bound opportunities that capture or convert resources at a particular moment. Proposed innovations whose applicability is timeless need close scrutiny.

- *A customer connection.* Most innovations are directly related to the individuals who will use them. They are then personal solutions, shaped by people who are very close to those with a need or a problem. Inventive solutions in search of problems and customers should raise a warning flag.

- *A disposition to act.* Most innovations do not begin with a prolonged planning process. They start with the making of a prototype—an early implementation of a new program design. If the innovation begins with a needs assessment or study phase, watch out!

Another distinction important to investors concerns the difference between *refinement* and *new-premise* innovations. Year after year, companies unveil their latest products, with improvements in versatility, durability, appearance, and other factors. This is refinement innovation—the ceaseless quest to make something better. Since one innovation often leads to another, this is best defined not as incremental but as progressive change. Sailing vessels, for example, have improved remarkably over hundreds of years through interrelated refinements in hull design, ballasts, and sail configurations. Yet the premise of wind power remained as a given. Similarly, programs supported by government have made important modifications to better serve people. While this is innovation with a small "i," the net effect of a five percent improvement here and ten percent gain there is a more effective product.

In contrast, an occasional innovation comes into being which contains at least one totally new premise. Thus, steam, diesel, and other engine propulsion systems came to ships as a totally new "givens" for an energy source. And in government grant programs, the premise of a business plan focused on outcomes—to replace a proposal focused on procedures—is gaining favor in some quarters, because it offers fundamental change.

To some extent, both refinement innovations and new-premise innovations follow the well-known paradigm shift concept of Thomas Kuhn. In his *Structure of Scientific Revolutions*, Kuhn speaks of the gradual refinement of a theory over time until a point when a new theory is introduced, which renders the old theory and the many assumptions built around it obsolete or inaccurate. [79] Refinements then continue until the next major new theory is introduced.

For investors, a value of the Kuhn context is the understanding that improvements over time will gradually come up against limits inherent in a basic premise. Sailing boats can never surpass their hull speed. Public programs built on accountability for procedures can never surpass the limitation that perfect procedural compliance does not guarantee perfect service to a customer. Until a threshold is reached, however, gradual improvements are the lifeblood of innovation. The key question for investors: Where is a project on the product, approach, or application development curve?

One departure from the Kuhn paradigm shift model is that a new innovation may not fully displace an older one. Thus, sailing vessels continued to thrive after motors were introduced, having moved from freight and passenger transport to recreational and sport applications. Further, the new premise innovation can actually enable more refinements in the old one. The greatest gains in sailing ship technology—to the point of producing a commercially viable sailing freight ship in the 1960s—happened *after* the introduction of motorboats! Some innovations may have elements of both types. Thus the catamaran design accepts wind power as a given, but does not accept the premise of a single hull.

Innovation and Planned Change

From the investment perspective, innovation has one clear meaning: it is a method for planned change. It is very different, however, from most approaches to change. Let's begin with that distinction.

When public programs, as well as the agencies that shape them, need improvement, the most popular solution, especially for a new leader, is reorganization. Whatever the perceived problems, the fault lies in structure. Energetic efforts lasting a year or more give birth to new circles and squares on a table of organization, along with new lines connecting them. An additional six months goes to moving offices and computers. At the end of the reorganization, ironically the most strongly felt impacts are not on customers but on staff. Uncertainties during reorganization tend to sap energies, and if anyone has an idea for trying out something new, the answer is, "Not now, we're reorganizing."

A second conventional change strategy is the study approach, often taking the form of a task force or blue-ribbon commission. After many meetings, the problem is defined and a course of action charted. Recommendations are likely to include the call for new money and a continuation of the group. When we ask of the outcome of the study, a ready answer is at hand: the study report. From the investor's perspective, the only acceptable outcome must be real change, not a document setting forth an agenda for change. Indeed, when planning and implementation are separated, the connection usually does not occur. The plan-and- study approach is supported by people-sensitive managers who see it as a vehicle for widespread participation, by research people who always believe that we always need more information, and by people who believe that studies are tantamount to action. [80]

A third common change strategy is the comprehensive new program. Following prolonged planning, a comprehensive new initiative is launched, generally designed to solve a big problem with a big solution. In many cases, the program is embodied in one or more large binders, with detailed instructions concerning all roles and operations.

Most big new programs fall short of their high expectations. One reason is that the many inferences made in planning for big programs (e.g., concerning customer behaviors in response to a service) will invariably prove incorrect. By the time key assumptions can be tested, it is too late. The mold is in place. Another problem is the presumption of inclusiveness. Regardless of how comprehensive they are, most programs are a good fit to some, but not all, customers.

These change strategies have three points in common. First, they are comprehensive, attempting to change many things at once. Second, they begin with and are driven by theory or concept; first the policy, then the practice. Third, they are based on structures and roles which remain intact over many changes in personnel.

Innovation as a method of planned change is very different. It begins by trying new things, watching results, and building on what works. As a change tool, innovation begins locally, focusing improvement on one problem or opportunity. It begins not with theory but with illustration. And it builds not on structures but on individuals who will lead change by their own example.

A related contrast concerns the relationship between policy and practice. For many years, public administration and management texts have portrayed policy-making as a rational and even linear process. In this view, policy is shaped by a problem-solving model that looks at options and conducts cost-benefit analyses to compare and select them. Increasingly, this view has been challenged as an inaccurate portrayal of the way things really work. As Lynn notes:

> Policy-making is less a matter of making good substantive choices on particular decisions than of designing and producing a continuing flow of less substantive actions with consequences attractive to relevant constituencies. [81]

Other observers go further. In their explicit "Assumptions for Innovation," The Innovation Group at The Rensselaerville Institute questions the adage that good practice should derive from good policy. A more useful sequence in many instances, this group believes, is to let policy follow practice. In this view, innovators as agents for change should not be as trained to act within existing policy. Their tinkering may well suggest new policies entirely.

Structuring the "Request for Innovations"

Throughout this book, we have underscored the point that investors will get what they request. If they ask for proposals, they will get need statements. If they define and request an Outcome Plan, they will get customer profiles and performance targets. In requesting applications for innovation projects, the key is to ask for information that will define the project as a tool for change. Consider this language from an Innovations Fund announcement by one state's Developmental Disabilities Planning Council:

> Innovation means more than just a new idea. It means a clear test of how a new approach can outperform a present practice. We are investing in the definition and testing of new approaches, not in ongoing services for people with developmental disabilities. Groups looking to fund current activities by adding the word "innovative" will not be well-served by this process.
>
> Innovations can include new approaches, new tools (including inventions), new enterprises, or virtually

anything else that can be shown to be important in improving present performance. [82]

One simple but effective framework for positioning innovations has been developed and tested over hundreds of projects by The Innovations Group at The Rensselaerville Institute. For this group, an innovation is best described as a response to these three questions:

1. *What's wrong?* What is it about existing programs and products that is proving ineffective? Alternatively, what is the gap or niche that existing products do not serve?

2. *What's new?* In terms of either a new premise or refinement, what do you propose to do that will eliminate or at least substantially relieve the condition you have described above as problematic? Please be very specific about the key features of your approach.

3. *What's the project?* What specific project will you undertake that will explicitly test the ability of your innovation to outperform present practices? Be highly specific about the results that you forecast, how they are different from the baseline of performance now achieved, and the products your innovation would improve or replace.

These three questions enable the investor to place a proposed innovation in a broader change context, starting with a baseline of present practices. [83]

In supporting innovations, it is tempting to move away from the investor focussing function defined in Chapter 6. How can we know from where creative juices will emerge? Since nothing is perfect, let innovation monies cast a wide

net. The problem with this philosophy is that innovation happening everywhere is often innovation going nowhere. Without a focus on one critical area needing change, innovations cannot build on each other. Also, the incidence of innovations applications tends to go up, not down, with the announcement of a delimited "sandbox" in which innovators may play. A boundary creates a challenge.
At the same time, the target need not be highly restrictive. From the Innovations Fund announcement quoted above comes this passage to define the sandbox:

> Innovations should address one or more of these three areas:
>
> - *Independence*—defined as the opportunity for people with disabilities to have and to make choices among realistic options;
>
> - *Productivity*—defined as either economic advancement for people with disabilities or the opportunity to make a contribution to other people and community life; and
>
> - *Integration*—defined as participation by people with developmental disabilities in community activities in which there is regular contact and interrelationship with people who are not disabled.
>
> In each case, the result should be a direct and tangible gain for people with a developmental disability.

In other cases, innovations may be much more closely targeted. Some may focus solely on efficiency—e.g., ways to lower current unit costs for a given level of result. Others may focus on effectiveness—providing more services for the same money.

The Innovation Payload

Many funders mistakenly believe that the desired outcome from innovative projects is the same as for other projects: an immediate gain in program services. While this may occur, it is a secondary benefit. The primary gain is the testing of a new approach that shows promise of outperforming a present practice. In this context, as much gain can accrue from a failure as from a success. Indeed, this is a clear exception to the investor's interest in ongoing services. It reverses the priorities between performance and information.

There are three possible end points for an innovations project. It can succeed, fail, or fizzle out. From the investor's viewpoint, only the fizzle—the failure to reach the finish line by doing everything possible to reach targets—is unacceptable.

Failures may actually yield a higher payload than success. When a program succeeds, we are tempted to accept it without question. Indeed, when adjustments in effective programs are proposed, the common response is, "Why tamper with a good thing?" As a result, many new programs that worked in an initial small application begin to fail when operated at a large scale without an understanding of the critical factors involved.

Failure, in contrast, attracts interest, although often for the wrong reasons. In our experience with hundreds of innovations projects, we have found that the most frequent outcome of a project that does not work is that other innovations are suggested which offer an increased likelihood of success. Even if no leads are forthcoming, one value remains. Many of the ideas that innovators test have been, at least peripherally, considered by an organization for some time. Such ideas clog a system with unresolved possibilities. A failed innovation at least enables the organization to move on.

The key to capturing the learning and change value of innovations is investor commitment to do something with innovative findings in hand. This is a critical matter, since the incidence of effective *spread* of innovations is probably more rarer than innovations themselves. The proportion of pilots, models, and demonstration projects that are never replicated at all is discouragingly high. Even a great idea in one context may not translate well to another. [84]

Two investor steps beyond project financing are critical. The first is to capture the informational value of the innovations project. The "Learning Plans" and "Lessons Learned" forums as discussed in Chapter 15 are essential practices. Project analysis must also address the question, "So what?" For those innovations that work on a small scale, what changes in larger policies and programs are suggested? To what activities and enterprises are both the findings and the innovation itself relevant?

When people gather to look at innovative project consequences, the energy can be very high, especially when compared to the concept-based meetings which consume so much time in and around government. Examples and illustrations are powerful drivers of both interest and commitments. Persons questioning this observation might think about the powerful ways in which beliefs are shaped by anecdotes far more than statistics.

While financial questions about cost per unit of result are important in all projects, they are critical in understanding the usefulness of an innovation. In times of shrinking public funds, the only way most innovations will be allowed to replace old practices will be if they save money. This can be a complex matter. For example, an innovation supported by a state may save money in an area that is fully reimbursed by the Federal government. Or its savings may only apply to additional customers, who states are not able to serve in any event. In both instances, savings may be significant but not motivating.

Cost analysis requires a separation of costs, to test the innovation and to calculate the costs for operations. Innovations must be very clear as to the portion of expenses that would not be present a) in expanded tests of the innovation, and b) in full implementation. Such financial distinctions should be identified by the investor as a way of sharpening the focus on what must be evident for the innovation to have a future. These distinctions then inform the performance targets.

The second step of *applying* learnings from an innovation must also be considered by investors as part of their work. Without this initiative, innovation findings are not likely to be used, no matter how clear and compelling they may be. The reasons for this come from a most useful body of research on diffusion of innovation conducted by Everett Rogers and colleagues. [85] This research has two key findings. First, innovations are much more effectively transmitted by a personal agent than by impersonal means, such as books and the electronic media. Further support for the original innovator to promote the personal approach will tend to yield higher return than investments to new people.

The second finding is that most people are simply not ready to try something new, even when someone else has proven that it works. The predisposition of humans to use an innovation begins with a very few "early adapters." These are people who like to go first. Then come the "mainstreamers," who will embrace a new practice only when it is has been shown to work by an early critical mass. Until that happens, no amount of information or documentation is likely to move them in that direction. Finally come the "laggards"—those who wish to be shown a hundred times and still are reluctant to change their behavior. Investors can find early adapters by shaping specific investment rounds which invite them to step forth and to apply an innovation. This strategy can be effectively combined with the personal agent theme. A successful innovator who is now responsible for five new applications of his/her approach is a powerful force for change.

The Research & Development Connection

One different but compatible way to look at innovation in the public sector is to consider its relationship to a major private-sector function called research and development. In the private sector, R & D is not an investment made for the sake of knowledge or academic image, or for the employment of futurists. Rather, it is born in this important fact: a product begins to become outdated the moment it is first introduced. Competition, new technologies (to reduce price as well as improve performance), and shifts in need and context are all factors contributing to obsolescence.

R & D has the purpose of defining, building, and testing specific new products which can be introduced *before* old products are totally outdated. Indeed, one measure of a high-performing company is that a significant portion of its revenues comes from products introduced in the past five years.

The contrast with government is instructive. In most public agencies, virtually no money is set aside for research and development to create and test new products. Rather, money is allocated to process activities—planning, task forces and a plethora of "blue-ribbon" commissions. Those employed in planning and research activities in public agencies can be counted upon to support this approach. The continuing refrain: we don't yet know enough to act.

This focus on paper rather than product is one reason that the same practices are repeated over many years. Thus we offer the same workshops, resource directories, multi-media campaigns, public housing programs, etc. that have been offered for years. We apparently believe that while the private sector must constantly introduce new products, government is doing nicely with the ones it has used for decades. Even if we don't believe this, no ready form of new program development appears evident.

Investor support of innovative projects can be seen as a vitally needed equivalent of the research and development function in industry. More specifically, innovative projects can be structured as key elements in the design process, which will test new approaches that government may then use widely or incorporate.

Thirty years ago, R & D was practiced in large and isolated research laboratories. A clear sequence of steps—from conceptual model to working representation to market entry—was practiced. This approach has now shifted dramatically, with the emphasis moving in two directions. One is the integration of development into the research process—building something as quickly as possible to prompt further research. The second is the use of small, more spontaneous product development teams connected to both manufacturing and sales environments which can replace research facilities purposefully set apart from other corporate functions.

The tool of R & D that has emerged from these shifts is called a prototype. A prototype is a working or functional representation of the product built in the early stages of development built for the purpose of testing key assumptions. The term is used in a wide variety of enterprises, from manufacturing to architecture. From the field of computer program development comes this typical description:

> Some people call mere screen and report mock-ups a prototype. Others mean a simulation, where data can be put in and fed back to the users, but without actual file accesses and processing taking place. That these mock-ups and simulations can be valuable for the user interface is one of the most important aspects of interactive systems design, and they give a much better indication of that interface than paper layout charts ever can. But they miss out on the full potential benefits of prototyping. Softwrite Systems uses the word "prototype" in the same way as the car industry does. You can climb into a prototype, switch it on, and drive it off. It is not the clay mock-up or the scale model you put in the wind tunnel; it is real and can give invaluable feedback on those aspects of the system that you need to choose to examine. [86]

Most prototypes involve customers directly, and are conducted within the settings in which the product will be used. Questions of benefit to and impacts on users, of product instruction and appearance, of field support and maintenance—all are understood at this point in the development process when there is plenty of time to respond.

Prototypes happen quickly, and are generally highly focused and relatively inexpensive. The point is to gain information by doing, not by thinking. When prototypes are completed, final design is completed, and a first generation of a product is introduced, generally in limited areas and quantities so that careful monitoring can take place. Test markets are generally selected to show the product to best advantage.

As with its counterpart in the private sector, the innovation prototype in government allows for testing of key assumptions of a new product on users or customers. And it provides a rich basis for establishing programs and policies on the basis of what is shown to work.

In the process methodologies now used for program development in the public sector, many inferences are made during planning. Some inferences are about what clients, patients, consumers and customers by other names need, want, and will use. Others are about how the program promotes or provokes change. When the master plan is finally complete and implementation begins, some of these critical assumptions will invariably break down. Sadly, this happens at a point in development far too late for ready course correction. Prototypes could have solved this problem.

As we consider prototyping for government, we must distinguish among terms that are often used interchangeably: they are *models, pilots,* and *demonstration projects*. In research and development, they are distinct.

When needed or at hand, models come first. Generally computer-based, they portray in a rigorous way the interaction among key variables. The principle is the same whether it is a simulation of the effects of wind and shape on the traction of a car, or the interaction of population migrations and capital reinvestment on a regional or national economy. While many of the diagrams that adorn planning documents and social and management science texts are advanced as "models," most lack such rigor. They are, at best, ways to describe things rather than to explain them.

Pilots and demonstration projects come *after* prototypes, not in place of them. They show initial use of the fully developed product, now presumed ready for application. Prototypes are made during design; pilots are made after it.

Investors may often find it useful to think of innovation projects as prototypes. This not only puts them into a design mold where later changes can be encouraged, but forces out a number of useful questions about the "product" itself. It also deals effectively with the matter of feasibility. If a government agency thought of trying a new approach, a common early step when dollars were more plentiful was to commission a feasibility study.

Prototypes can be seen as a different way of looking at feasibility. Innovation projects can be structured as feasibility tests which are both less costly and more predictive than are feasibility *studies.* [87]

Investor Guidelines

We close with 12 guidelines to investors in innovations. They are based on tested assumptions for innovation. [88]

1. *Be willing to place your bets on individuals.* Innovation does not come from books, budgets, or plans. It comes from individuals who have a vision for a better way and the project to express it. Innovation is rarely pre-formed in a tidy and complete program description. Its potential is better gauged by the presence of one or more people who are highly knowledgeable about alternatives to the status quo and who have the persistence to reach their goal.

2. *Be prepared to invest in some unruly people.* Innovators may not make ideal supplicants. They can be irritatingly self-assured. Their need for achievement may well dominate their need for affiliation, and they may gain their energy by having been fired or rejected by someone else. Remember, you are choosing an innovator, not an employee. The same traits that would lead to prompt rejection for

hiring may prove essential in sustaining a difficult innovation. Remember George Bernard Shaw's comment: "The reasonable man adapts himself to the world; the unreasonable one persists in trying to adapt the world to himself. Therefore, all progress depends on the unreasonable man."

3. *Look for entrepreneurial characteristics.* Ask would-be innovators about past failures and listen carefully. Do they blame their failures on external forces, or look squarely at their own mistakes? Did they learn from their errors or not? Ask about risk as the innovators see it. Do they distinguish between uncertainty (which they do not control and wish to minimize) and risk (which they can at least manage and calculate)? How sustainable is their energy? Above all, look at behavior. The innovator's past actions (i.e., at starting things and carrying them to completion) are a far more useful predictor than their words about the future.

4. *Ensure that money for innovations is available on a prompt and flexible basis.* On the one hand, investors need not have large pools of money available to encourage innovation. Indeed, more innovation comes from bootstrapping rather than from a rich resource base. On the other hand, energetic individuals with time-bound opportunities cannot wait six months for a decision and another six months to get funds. And they cannot work with a tightly-proscribed line-item budget that cannot be adjusted. Contracting guidelines for conventional projects can stop innovators dead in their tracks.

5. *Give as much weight to those innovations which are not anchored in theory as to those which are.* Innovations may well precede conceptual develop-

ment. In technology, for example, many of the most important 20th-century innovations began with an individual with a hunch, who had the ability to try it out. Innovations involve insight and intuition that cannot be understood in an analytical context. Some are not well understood until completed.

6. *Don't get hung up on what constitutes an innovation and what does not.* Definitional pursuits of such topics as "newness" quickly become red herrings. Instead, structure questions so that the response positions the project as an innovation in terms of change. Also, be strongly guided by projected results. Finally, look for characteristics known to be associated with many innovations. One is a focus on opportunities, not on problems. If a project must be done now to capture some time-bound conditions, it is more likely an innovation than if it is an idea perennially applicable.

7. *Avoid multi-person, multi-criteria review processes which are likely to eliminate some of the most divergent and promising of innovations.* One strongly supportive reviewer who feels that the innovation deserves a chance (for reasons they may or may not fully articulate) is worth more than a tepid consensus. The sharpest innovations are often eliminated in the committee processes. In terms of criteria, "reasonableness" and "feasibility" as seen by reviewers are not relevant to innovations, even if the reviewers are experts in the field. Fred Smith received a C from his Ivy League professor for the paper that profiled what later became Federal Express. The main criticism: his idea was not realistic.

8. *Let the innovation be a start-up.* Innovators need independence, and often cannot start or even end

within organizational frameworks. As long as it is not costly to do so, encourage independent initiative. If the innovation does take place within an organization, make it a condition of your investment that the sponsoring group grant the innovation deferment from procedural compliance. Further, let the innovator operate without monitoring. Use an occasional milestone and a focus on results for accountability. Remember, the payload is information and learning, not service.

9. *Structure your investment to give the innovators whatever entrepreneurial framework they may need.* Such a framework may include performance-based compensation or bonuses, clear personal responsibility, and clear ways to keep score. You can also add protection that the innovator is locked into the deal. While the venture capital approach of asking the entrepreneurs to pledge their home and car as collateral is not appropriate, innovators may well be willing to lend personal resources to their enterprise.

#10. *Rather than to set aside innovations that are deemed too risky, work with implementors to reduce risk.* In many cases, risk is a matter of scale and can be handled by reducing the project to a more manageable size. Most innovators won't mind. Their interest is in trying out the idea and they are surprisingly willing to accept compromise as long as something can be tried. When the risk is known, ask yourself, "What's the worst thing that could happen if this project fails?" If you can live with the answer, proceed! (At the same time, give no added consideration to a project simply because it has a high risk. Risk, like novelty, is a side effect of some innovations, not a definer of them.)

#11. *Be prepared to stay with your innovation selections once they are made.* While many projects flourish with funder indifference, innovations should not lightly be abandoned. Innovators may face unexpected barriers and your help in surmounting them can be critical. Indeed, some projects should be seen as partnerships, in which the investor must be prepared to play an active role to deal with obstacles that implementors cannot, by themselves, overcome. Another form of involvement may be progressively greater support while a project remains in a fragile start-up mode. An initial $10,000, three-month project may then deserve a $50,000, twelve-month project in order to work itself into final form and impact.

#12. *With the differences discussed, recognize that the framework of the full Outcome plan remains relevant.* Indeed, the emphasis on a tight definition of the product and the connection to customers are especially valid with innovations. Innovations are often characterized by very clear premises, while driven by an evident problem of people whose needs are not well met by existing products. At the same time, not all innovations projects should be required to offer great detail. If an innovations project had all the answers, it would not be there in the first place.

Where innovation is needed, funders are in the catbird seat. More than almost any other group in American life, they tend to get what they promote. In many ways, the most critical contribution grantmakers can make is actually not money. It is a discipline about innovation that recognizes that the search for genuine alternatives to present practice requires very different tools than the support of on-going programs. Innovation is a core premise, not an add-on component. Innovation involves an explicit test of a new approach, not a massaging of dreams or visions.

Buying change is possible. But one needs the coin of that realm.

62. Drucker, Peter, *Innovation and Entrepreneurship.* New York: Harper and Row, 1985.

63. Schumpeter, J.A., *The Theory of Economic Development.* Cambridge: Harvard University Press, 1934.

64. Quinn, James Brian, "Technological Innovation, Entrepreneurship, and Strategy," *Sloan Management Review*, Spring, 1979.

65. Whitsett, David A. and Yorks, Lyle, *From Management Theory to Business Sense.* New York: American Management Association, 1983.

66. For each entrepreneurial characteristic,one or more tests presumed to measure its presence. In the case of personal responsibility, a primary tool is Rotter's I.-E. Locus of Control Scale. It is designed to designate people as "externals" or "internals" in terms of relative weight they give to outside factors in explaining the result of their actions.

67. Given that the entrepreneur's behavior is more important than his or her words, situations are often established in which actions can be observed. For risk taking, for example, would-be entrepreneurs are offered cash for their performance at a ring toss game. They make little money for close-up easy tosses, moderate money for a challenging mid-range toss and large money for a very long toss. Successful entrepreneurs tend to work in the middle ground—between certainty and chance. This, in turn, is generally interpreted as reflecting

an internal locus of control as defined in footnote 66. They choose the middle peg because it is the only one where skill matters.

68. For an elaboration, see: Albert Shapero, "The Role of Entrepreneurial Research at the Less than National Level," Office of Economic Research, U.S., Department of Commerce. 1977.

69. Cited in Shapero, 1977.

70. This and other fascinating profiles of innovators are reported in Ethlie Ann Vare and Greg Ptacek, *Mothers of Invention.* New York: William Morrow, 1988.

71. Quotes are from Bill Berkowitz, *Local Heroes.* Boston: Lexington Books, 1987. The book covers 20 individuals who met community needs by starting something. The profiles and words of these individuals are remarkably congruent with entrepreneurs in other areas.

72. Berkowitz, 1987.

73. Kanter, Rosabeth Moss, *The Change Masters.* New York: Simon and Schuster, 1983.

74. Bennis, Warren and Nanus, Burt, *Leaders: The Strategy for Taking Charge.* New York: Harper and Row, 1985.

75. Schrage, Michael, *Shared Minds.* New York: Random House, 1990. Given the conventional stress upon entrepreneurs as soloists, this book is most helpful in showing how and why duos, trios and quartets can make equally beautiful music.

76. This tongue in cheek profile is in: William B. Gartner, "The Entrepreneur or the Self Made Man," Center for Entrepreneurial Studies, University of Virginia. (undated working paper.)

77. Webber, Alan M. , "Corporate Egoists Gone with the Wind,", *The Wall Street Journal*, April 15, 1991. Webber is editorial director of the Harvard Business Review.

78. Drucker, 1985.

79. Kuhn, Thomas S., *The Structure of Scientific Revolutions*. Chicago: University of Chicago Press, 1962.

80. An extreme example of the "study as answer" approach recently came to our attention. It is a workplan for a federal agency on supported employment for persons with a disability. Here's how it begins:

OBJECTIVE I: *To impact the quantity and quality of training available to personnel in supported employment by 9/30/92.*

1.1 Establish Blue Ribbon Task Force (BRTF-1) for objective implementation.

It continues through eight objectives, each to be achieved through formation of another BRTF!

81. Lynn, Laurence E. , Jr., *Managing Public Policy*. Boston: Little Brown, 1987.

82. This passage is from request for innovation plans from the New York State Disabilities Planning Council issued in the summer of 1990.

83. Persons with a strong interest in innovation with public organizations may wish to subscribe to the national quarterly, ***INNOVATING***. The Rensselaerville Institute, Rensselaerville, New York, 12147, (518) 797-3783.

84. The impressive performance of Federal Express in the U.S. for example, has not been effectively spread to Europe and other nations despite many millions of dollars devoted to this innovation diffusion.. The company's core tenets of central control and constant timetables have had great difficulty in surmounting other cultural traditions. (See "Federal Express Finds its Pioneering Formula Falls Flat Overseas," in *The Wall Street Journal*, April 15, 1991.)

85. The seminal book is Everett M. Rogers, *Diffusion of Innovation*. New York: The Free Press, 1982.

86. Tozer, Jane E., "Prototyping as a Systems Development Methodology: Opportunities and Pitfalls," *Information and Software Tech*, Vol. 29, No. 5.

87. Peters and Waterman in their seminal book *In Search of Excellence* (New York: Harper and Row, 1982) spoke to feasibility determination cost in this way:

> Experimentation acts as a form of cheap learning for most of the excellent companies, usually proving less costly—and more useful—than sophisticated market research or careful staff planning.

MIT's Frank P. Davidson adds this thought on accuracy:

A project does not become feasible because someone has predicted that it will be; it is made feasible by the actual willingness of individuals and organizations to undertake binding commitments (on the basis of, among other things, such predictions). *Technology Review*, December, 1971.

88. These guidelines are grounded in some tested assumptions concerning innovation and its differences from other functions. A useful reference is *Assumptions for Innovation*, The Innovation Group, The Rensselaerville Institute, Rensselaerville, NY, 1990.

AFTERWORD

The practice of proposal preparation and review is an industry. It is perpetuated through books, conferences, case studies, and general practice. If the Outcome Funding approach is to effectively become established as an ongoing enterprise, it needs its own critical mass of thinking, doing, and disseminating. Our hope is that readers of this book will be prompted to forge that foundation.

Here are a few thoughts for how this can be done.

Research

A research agenda for Outcome Funding needs pursuit. Public administration and policy centers, both academically- and government-based, must recognize the importance of grant-making as a key public sector function. They must also see funding not as a mechanical process which is so cut and dried that it defies productive scrutiny, but as a rich source of improvement and change. Indeed, the failure to raise fundamental questions about resource use outside of the organization is one reason that externally-directed funds are as procedurally driven in most public agencies as are internal allocations.

Questions are bountiful:

- What assumptions of private-sector investors for forecasting enterprise success are relevant to government project investments?
- What are the precedents for the introduction of

personal judgment in a public function?

- What are the implications of "equity" and "fairness" based not on uniform and impersonal analysis, but on tailored and personal understanding?

- What questions about the dual roles of government as provider and enforcer are raised by the shift to the Outcome Funding perspective?

- What are the conditions under which the innovation option to financing of new approaches should be employed?

While Outcome Funding can take root without good answers to these questions, the continued development of a conceptual framework is needed for its widespread acceptance.

Documentation

Outcome Funding needs information about present practice which can only come from those who use it. In a surprising number of instances, documentation need not be onerous. Consider time expended by the grant-making agency. A simple but useful tool is a slip stapled to each copy of each proposal reviewed in a given grant cycle. All individuals who touch that copy are asked to log in, noting the elapsed time the copy was in their possession and the actual time expended in reading or evaluating the document. This kind of data develops baseline information not only on unit costs per proposal, but also per funded proposal. This enables us to understand the patterns and variations across many agencies, kinds of funding situations and problems.

Documentation of costs by applicants in the current process is equally important. How many person-days go into a proposal's preparation, and what proportion of proposals submitted are actually funded? Broader questions arise concerning the strengths and drawbacks, as seen by implementors. To what extent, for example, do grant recipients focus on work plan compliance rather than on results in reports to the funder?

Current benefits are another area for documentation. One straightforward question to gauge effectiveness: How many of the projects funded would not have been supported if results were known in advance? Unless this number is negligible, the wisdom of seeking a better selection device is clear.

When Outcome Funding is used, documentation becomes comparative. How does the business plan and Due Diligence processes compare in selection and tracking cost with proposals and their review? How do results of projects selected through each approach differ? Does Outcome Funding realize the improvements in project management which it seeks? Outcome Funding must live or die by its own performance.

Product Improvement

Outcome Funding can also take its own definitional medicine. Consider it as a product. It has a specific use—increasing the productivity of government agencies who finance others to achieve their purposes. It presumably has reasonably clear instructions and product features that differentiate it from its competitor, proposal development and grading. Over time, it may even develop performance warranties. Well and good. Probably the greatest advantage of product thinking, however, is product development.

The development of new designs and prototypes for Outcome Funding will largely be done by its customers. As people and agencies experiment with ways to introduce the outcome mindset, they will discover and define new tools and practices. Groups experimenting with ROTI (return on taxpayer investment), milestone management, and all other concepts discussed in this book will go well beyond our own thinking.

Another form of product improvement is the discovery of new applications. Our sense, for example, is that the outcome approach can be applied to functions within organizations as well as beyond them. If an agency is preparing to launch a new program or commission a task force, for example, it can ask the initiators to develop their thinking as a business plan. The elements of performance targets, customers, and product definition are all relevant. Indeed, business plans can be applied to such routine activities as a monthly staff meeting.

We do urge constant attention to one vulnerability of our approach. To the extent that we lose our sense of open-mindedness and allow our approach to become too codified or sanctified, we run the danger of replacing one dogma with another. We must not let Outcome Funding become another form of funding by methodology.

Communication

None of these steps matter unless experience and results are communicated such that others may learn from them. The Innovation Group of The Rensselaerville Institute will serve as an agent for the diffusion of Outcome Funding tools and techniques. Think of us as the learning bank for Outcome Funding. Please make us your repository for experience and ideas. The more extensive the deposits, the more resources become available for use by others. This is one bank that will not go broke from withdrawals!

About the Authors

Harold S. Williams is President of The Rensselaerville Institute, a development institution whose business is organizational and community renewal. He has served as lead consultant to a number of change projects. His clients have included the US Presidential Commission, the Health Innovation Fund of Ontario Province, Canada, and over forty public agencies throughout the US. He is also editor of ***INNOVATING*** magazine.

Arthur Y. Webb is the Chief Executive Officer of the Village Centers of Care, Village Nursing Home, New York, NY. He was formerly a Research Professor in the Heller Graduate School for Social Policy and the Institute for Health Policy at Brandeis University. He was (and is) also the first Fellow of Innovation of The Rensselaerville Institute and has served as chairman and member of many public commissions and councils.

William J. Phillips directs The Innovation Group at The Rensselaerville Institute. Under his leadership this center has become known both nationally and internationally. It enables organizations, public and private, large and small, to introduce and adopt new mindsets and approaches for improving organizational and personal effectiveness.